PRAISE FOR *WIND AND WHIRLWIND*

This is truly an inspirational and immensely helpful book. David Moffett- Moore lived through one of the most difficult experiences a pastor can possibly endure. By reflecting deeply on his own personal crisis in ministry, he has written a wonderful guide for other pastors as well as for those who care about them. While this book will benefit clergy immensely, it will also serve as a great resource for members of congregations as well. In this relatively short book, he provides a cogent analysis of current ecclesiastical realities and their impact upon clergy. However, this book does not stop with analysis. Through the simple meditations he suggests and the questions he provides, David Moffett- Moore offers all of his readers useful tools for personal growth and understanding. In doing so, he makes a major contribution to clergy-congregation relationships. This is a significant book!

Rev. Dr. Robert R. LaRochelle
Pastor, Second Congregational Church, UCC, Manchester, CT

For clergy who have time to read only one book on congregational conflict, it should be *Wind and Whirlwind*. After providing a concise, but thorough, summary of cultural changes and their impact on congregational life, Moffett-Moore offers wise counsel on practices congregations and their leaders can adopt to manage any conflict that may emerge, from its inception. Couched within a description of Moffett-Moore's own personal experience of finding himself at the center of congregational conflict as a pastor, and peppered with the illustrations one would expect of a good preacher, *Wind and Whirlwind* is thoroughly engaging and readable. An excellent resource both for clergy and for use with congregational leaders.

Rev. Lolly Dominski
President, Academy of Parish Clergy
Morton Grove Community Church, Presbyterian, Morton Grove, Illinois
PhD Candidate in Liturgical Studies,
Garrett-Evangelical Theological Seminary

David Moffett-Moore's book, *Wind and Whirlwind* is a thoughtful and inspiring manuscript. The questions at the end for reflection and meditation offer an important spiritual grounding consistent with kinds of practices that allow clergy to cope with these types of challenges. At some point in their careers, most clergy hit a snag in their ministries and become the focus of their congregation's angst. David does an excellent job of describing this overwhelming and devastating experience with candor and grace. But the most important thing he does is to role model how to get grounded when this happens, how to find support, how to take responsibility for the growth opportunity this presents and how to continue to lead in the midst of managing one's own feelings. This should be required reading for all clergy early in their careers.

Susan Nienaber
Senior Consultant
The Alban Institute

No mere armchair advice. As a pastor who has survived the storms of conflict, David Moffett-Moore provides bearings and invites you to celebrate. "Most jobs have a 'to do' list. Ministry has a 'to be' list." Moffett-Moore models authentic "spiritual calisthenics"—practices to reorient your own body, mind and spirit for serving well.

Rev. Dr. Kent Ira Groff, APC
retreat leader, spiritual companion
and author of Clergy Table Talk and Honest to God Prayer

To Bill,
To a Fellow Pilgrim
on the Way!
David

WIND AND WHIRLWIND

BEING A PASTOR
IN A STORM OF CHANGE

BY DAVID MOFFETT-MOORE, APC

Conversations in Ministry Series
Robert D. Cornwall, APC, Editor

Energion Publications
Gonzalez, FL
2013

Cover Design: Nick May

ISBN10:   1-938434-55-2
ISBN13:   978-1-938434-55-6
Library of Congress Control Number: 2013932756

Energion Publications
P. O. Box 847
Gonzalez, FL 32560

850-525-3916

energionpubs.com

ACKNOWLEDGEMENTS

Every play has a cast and every story has its characters. This book was inspired by the true story of our life together at St. Peter's United Church of Christ, Frankfort Illinois. I am grateful to the congregation and their willingness to work together with me as their pastor. Together, we found a way to become a glad and resilient church, as described later. I am grateful for their trust, determination and especially their friendship.

This book would not exist without the members of the Academy of Parish Clergy, their sponsorship of this series and the advice and encouragement they have offered. This is especially true for Rev. Dr. Bob Cornwall, series editor, and Rev. Dr. Kent Ira Groff, author of the first volume. I've long dreamed of being an author. They harnessed that dream and made it a reality.

My father, Rev. John Moore, continues to be my mentor who guides and inspires me. My wife, Becki, has been more than companion and friend through these years. Her listening ear and supporting spirit have been more nourishing than food or drink.

Every play needs an audience and every book a reader, so I acknowledge you, the reader. Without you, this would only be an exercise in self-examination and reflection. I hope this sharing of my story will inspire you to be more than a reader, motivate you to actively participate in your congregation's story and encourage you to stay the course and finish the task.

TABLE OF CONTENTS

SERIES PREFACE

Parish ministry can be an exciting and challenging vocation. This has always been the case, but it is perhaps even truer today. At least in the European and North American contexts, institutional forms of religion are finding themselves pushed to the sidelines. Their purpose and value has been questioned, and with these questions come further questions about the professional status of those who are called to serve these congregations.

A generation ago, congregational ministers might see themselves as members of a professional class, similar to that of medical doctors and attorneys. The Academy of Parish Clergy, the sponsor of this book series, was founded with just that vision – to encourage and enhance the professional practice of parish ministry. This was to be accomplished by setting professional standards, including the encouragement to engage in regular continuing education, and then providing a means of accountability to those standards. Although the broader culture has raised questions about the professional standing of parish clergy, the need for professional standards, continuing education, and accountability remains as important today as ever before. This is because the world in which ministry is being done is ever changing, and therefore clergy must adapt, learn new skills, and reposition themselves for a new day. It is helpful, therefore, to walk in the company of others who are also engaged in similar kinds of ministry.

What makes parish ministry both exciting and challenging is that most clergy are generalists. They're like the family practitioner, dealing with a wide variety of issues and people. No day is exactly the same, for they serve as teachers, preachers, worship leaders, providers of pastoral care, administrators, and social justice leaders. They may be more gifted in some areas than others, but ultimately they find themselves engaged in a wide variety of tasks that often push them to the limits of ability and endurance. It is not a vocation that can be undertaken on one's own, and for a variety of reasons parish ministers need to find a community of others who share this calling, so that they might find encouragement, support, and ideas for dealing with parish life and ministry in the broader world.

Part of the founding vision of the Academy of Parish Clergy was to facilitate this need to find a community of peers, and with this in mind Academy members were encouraged to create and join together in Colleague Groups, where they could encourage one another and explore issues that confront clergy in their daily ministry, often using the "Case Study Method," which was emerging at the time among the professions. That model is still available, but it is the hope of the editors of this series that these books will also provide a foundation for conversation in clergy groups.

This vision continues to sustain the Academy more than forty years after its founding, and the new APC book series, *Conversations in Ministry*, seeks to extend this vision by offering to clergy books written primarily by practicing clergy for practicing clergy dealing with the issues that confront them in ministry today. Each book, published in partnership with Energion Publications, will be brief and focused (under 100 pages). Each book is designed to encourage reflection and conversation among clergy. The editors and authors of these books hope that the books will be taken up by groups of clergy and inspire conversation.

It is important to point out the use of the preposition "in." The conversations that are envisioned here are not simply about ministry, but are designed to emerge from within the context of ministry. While the initial book in the series covered a variety of important issues facing clergy, in this the second volume in this series, we are led directly into what can be for clergy one of the most debilitating experiences of ministry — congregational conflict. As was true in the first volume, this book will reflect the purpose of the series, but each author will take the conversation in the direction the topic suggests.

May this series of books be a blessing to all who read them.

Robert D. Cornwall, APC
General Editor

ORIENTATION

Orienteering is a well established and respected element of the Scouting program. It requires that the Scout be able to find his or her position and identify and follow a path using only a map and compass. It requires a variety of skills: ability to read a map, use a compass, measure one's pace, find and follow a route through changing and rough terrain. In order to become a first class Scout, one must prove one's skill in orienteering.

Being a first class pastor is much like this. It requires competency in a variety of skills, ability to use limited resources and read mixed signals to find a position and follow a path through rough, unknown terrain. It is my hope that this book will offer some level of confidence in pastoral orienteering, making it through the rough patches to find the smooth path ahead.

That which is most personal is also often what's most universal. Beginning with my experience of being a pastor in crisis serving a parish in crisis and building on this through the research and training it motivated, this volume will help pastors care for their congregations living through times of overwhelming change as well as cope with their congregations when times of conflict occur. Using my experience as a thread, I will weave a story offering survival and the opportunity of success.

Our culture is enduring a time of epochal change. Change leads to stress and stress leads to conflict. As individuals, we breathe an atmosphere of anxiety. If our congregations are to survive, we must find ways to endure the change, defend ourselves from the stress, and resolve the conflict in ways that can lead to stronger, healthier congregations. We need to become resilient.

This book's title is inspired by Hosea 8:7, "They that sow the wind shall reap the whirlwind." In many ways, it feels like we are enduring a whirlwind of conflict and change, in our culture and in our congregations. Yet it was from this whirlwind that God spoke to Job and God only appeared to Elijah after the earthquake, wind and fire. There is a way through, a presence in the midst and a goal ahead. Together, we can find them!

Each chapter offers a concise lesson, includes a meditation, and offers questions for reflection and discussion. The book is intended to be used as a springboard for conversation among clergy groups. It is one in a series of such books offered jointly by the Academy of Parish Clergy and Energion Publications.

I

November 11, 2007

I was more nervous than I'd been in years: frightened, scared, terrified. I had no idea what would happen next. I could not concentrate on what I was doing or anticipate my next steps. I hadn't slept well in weeks. Becki and I had talked and planned and prayed, but nothing was settled. Fear, not faith, was my constant companion.

It was Sunday, November 11, 2007. We were having our regular quarterly Congregational Meeting, but there was nothing regular about this meeting. I stood behind the lectern, bracing myself for whatever might happen next. Clearing my throat and trying to look brave, staring down the congregation, I began what was listed as my Pastor's Report.

"The Church Council has asked for my resignation. I have agreed to their terms, including a three month notice. I will no longer be your pastor as of March 1, 2008. Thank you for the honor of serving as your pastor these past four years. I wish you all the best and pray that God may guide you in your next steps."

I don't think very many heard the last two sentences. After the first two sentences, there was a cry of uproar from the congregation, which was hearing this for the first time, shouts asking questions and some demanding the resignation of the Council. It was chaos. Still shaking, I sat down to let the Council President sort it all out. As Council President, he chaired the Congregational Meeting. He was also the face of the loyal opposition. I had no idea who or how many were behind him seeking my resignation or how many might support me if it came to a floor fight. I certainly had not expected that the floor fight we hoped to avoid would become so tangible a reality.

Different denominations have different ways of dealing with church conflict. The United Church of Christ allows for a very strong congregational polity. The local church owns all its property, selects its own pastor, writes its own constitution and by-laws, establishes its own requirements for membership, etc. By simple majority vote, it can leave the denomination at any duly called congregational meeting. Each congregation is independent, while in covenant with one another. I call it "defiantly autonomous." I grew up in a Methodist parsonage, a denomination with a much more hierarchical structure. Coming to the United Church of Christ was both a breath of fresh air and a leap into chaos.

I was born in 1953, ordained in 1976 and have had employment since I was eleven years old, secular or sacred. I had never been fired. As a pastor in a parsonage, I was also losing my home and all my contacts with people whom I had regarded as friends. When a pastor loses his or her position, it has shattering effects that are emotional and spiritual as well as financial. The money may be the least of worries.

The church I'd been serving for the past four years was a grand historic church that had a great heritage, a beautiful sanctuary where hundreds gathered weekly for worship, a pipe organ for a space twice as large as they had, and a history of large Sunday school classes. Historically, the local mayor was almost always a member of the church. It was a church that seemed to have more glory days behind it than before it, had decreased while the community had increased and was not sure of its destiny. It was also a church that had fired five of its previous seven pastors.

The Council President restored order and I regained some semblance of composure. The question was put by the congregation to me was whether or not I was willing to stay. I replied that I felt I needed to comply with the will of the Council. In any case, given the state of the congregation, we would need to obtain the services of a church consultant to help us work through this crisis.

A petition was circulated around the congregation which gained the signatures of nearly all our active members. The Council rescinded its request for my resignation, and six of the twelve Council members resigned from the Council. By the time all the dust had settled, we lost five of our three hundred families. Some who had been active became less so and some who had not been active became more so. We contracted with the Alban Institute, which met with most of our membership individually or in groups over a three month period and presented an in-depth report of their findings. They also provided a lengthy and detailed paper documenting their work and recommending next steps.

That February I left for a month's sabbatical to stay with my brother-in-law's family in Hawaii. If you're going to be homeless — why not Hawaii? I took with me a dozen books on stress management, conflict resolution, dealing with disagreeable people, etc. I eventually read every book and watched every video the Alban Institute recommended and enrolled in a Clergy Clinic course offered by the Lombard Mennonite Peace Center. I shared with pastors whose wisdom I respected and whose opinions I trusted. I found a life vest and safety rope in the Academy of Parish Clergy, an independent national ecumenical organization of, by and for parish clergy organized for mutual support, encouragement and accountability. In short, I checked the "all the above" option.

I found out that I am not the only one. I found out that most congregations are living in stress and dealing with some low level of conflict on an ongoing basis and that it flares up every three to five years. I found out that most clergy are stressed. The stress means we are always living with some level of anxiety, and there are long term negative consequences. The stress and conflict leads to a question of call: on the part of the pastor, a question of call to this congregation and to ministry in general; on the part of the congregation, a question of identity, purpose and meaning.

It is good to remember that there are positive benefits to stress. Stress simply means there is more than one force at work in our lives, more than one priority, and more than one perspective. It is good to have more than one idea in the room at one time! No trapeze artist or tight rope walker would endeavor to work in a stress free environment; stress is necessary for the artist to swing and to hold the rope taut for the walk. We need a healthy tension, but we need a tension that is truly healthy.

There must be a better way!

MEDITATION

Look back over the events of your life. When have you been most frightened, most fearful? As a young child? As a youth? As an adult? Put yourself back into those situations. Remember how it feels to be afraid. How does it affect you physically, your heart rate, etc.? How does it affect your ability to think and to focus?

When we are truly afraid, it is hard to feel anything but that fear.

QUESTIONS FOR REFLECTION AND CONVERSATION

1. Look over the events described above, how do those events compare? How does the fear you experienced in those events compare? How did you respond in those events? Looking back, are there other ways you could have responded? How would a different response have affected the outcomes? What did you learn about yourself in those events?

2. What was the first crisis you faced in your ministry? What were the events that led up to that crisis? Describe how you handled it? What might you have done differently? How would it have helped? What resources were helpful to you?

3. Often in crisis, we feel most alone. What support was helpful to you, personally, professionally and spiritually?

2

UNIQUE, LIKE EVERYONE ELSE

It was February of 2008. The congregation had formed a steering committee to select a church consultant to help us work through issues we'd rather avoid. It was going to be tough work, but we had determined to get through it together. I had made a quick get-away to gain some personal respite. I needed a chance to catch my breath, to rest up before all the heavy work ahead. I had picked a good cover.

I had joined the Academy of Parish Clergy the previous fall, just as the storm was breaking with the Church Council. The promotional material looked interesting and I figured I would need all the help I could get. Their annual conference was to be at a retreat center in Florida. They were bringing together judicatory representatives from different denominations to discuss the state of the church.

When you live in the Chicago area, February in Florida sounds good. The conference theme meant I'd find some help for my local situation. The retreat center meant I'd get to rest my soul a while.

Margaret Mead spoke of our individuality somewhere, saying "You are unique, just like everyone else."

Part of the stress I felt was due to my feeling that I was going through something no one else had experienced. My church council had asked for my resignation! We'd had a verbally explosive congregational meeting! I didn't know who to trust! I didn't know what would happen next! We were entering an intense time with an expensive consultant! We were going to be challenged in ways we'd not been before, urged to be more open and honest with one another. Could we handle it? Would we be up to the challenge?

No one had been this exposed! No one had been this threatened! No one had been this frightened!

As a first time participant, members of the Academy took time getting to know me. One by one, the elders of the group, the long-term members, asked about my background, experiences and expectations. One by one, I was given the cherished knowledge that I was not the only one. Others had travelled this road before me, others had been through this wilderness, and had found their way to the other side.

I was unique, like everyone else.

Congregations face critical issues on a regular, cyclical basis. Every three to five years there will be a presenting issue to be dealt with. It can be ignored, repressed, dealt with subconsciously or faced honestly. Often, the pastor becomes the bellwether, the lightning rod, even the scapegoat. Too often, the way the pastor and congregation deal with the issue is to change partners. Sometimes, after the pastor has faced this crisis, taken it personally, moved on, and then faced it all again, the pastor stops being a pastor. Clergy burn-out is an ongoing concern and a tragic consequence.

The July 25, 2012 issue of *Christian Century* cites a study by Pastoral Care, Inc, that over seventeen hundred pastors leave the ministry every month (p.8). This is an enormous exodus and a clear sign of a major problem that needs to be addressed.

I view my father, a retired pastor, and his generation as a generation of "Lone Rangers," pastors who faced their crises as lonely warriors or lone sentinels. This may not be fair or accurate, but it is based on my observations growing up in a parsonage. Lone pastors, whether rangers or warriors or sentinels, do not ask for help; they deal with issues as they come up as best they can without expecting assistance or anticipating appreciation. It is all just part of the job.

The truth is none of us are ever alone. If I believe our ecclesiology, if I believe in the priesthood of believers and the great cloud of witnesses, if I believe Paul when he says, "It is no longer I who live, but Christ Jesus who lives in me," then I also know that we are never alone, no matter how "alone" I might feel. The church is the body of Christ; we are the flesh and blood filled with his spirit. Christ is the head of the church, which is his body. We are his presence here and now, in our time and our place. The church is not just a human institution, but a spiritual fellowship and organization established by God. As such, it shall exist to the end of time and even the gates of Hell cannot prevail against it, or our current congregational conflict. As a member of the body of Christ, I am in spiritual fellowship with all Christians in all times and places. We are all one in Christ!

My experience at the conference, with other pastors sharing their stories and listening to mine offered a process that eased my burden and reminded me of what I already knew. It made this intellectual assent to be a lived experience.

I am not the only one who has faced a crisis in ministry, not the only one who had challenges that felt insurmountable or faced dilemmas for which I could find no answers. Other people have gone before me. There is a path I can choose to follow and guides eager to help. It may be a wilderness, but there is a way through!

MEDITATION

Imagine being alone in a house on a dark and stormy night: lightning flashing, thunder booming, wind howling. Sense that aloneness. When have you felt that before? What was the storm raging outside and the fear clinging inside?

Now imagine the breaking dawn of a new day, with the sun rising over the horizon and light chasing away the shadows. Remember how the air smells after a storm clears. Feel that relaxation.

QUESTIONS FOR REFLECTION AND CONVERSATION

1. At what time in your life have you felt most alone? How did you get through that period? What resources did you find helpful? Were there others who came to accompany you?

2. What support groups are you actively involved with? How have you benefited from them?

3. How has a desire to be unique expressed itself in your life? Has it led to a sense of being alone? How have you dealt with this in your spirituality?

3

EVERYTHING CHANGES, NOTHING REMAINS

Heraclitus was a pre-Socratic philosopher who lived in what is now Turkey. Very little of what he wrote is available to us. He wrote largely using aphorisms and sayings, leaving much to the interpretation of the reader. His philosophy included the idea that everything is in a state of flux: that reality is about the flow rather than any static, unchanging state.

One of his sayings is "One can never step twice into the same river." The water that I put my first foot in is different from the water that I put my second foot in. Even from the time of one step to the other, the water has changed. Another way he puts it is, "Everything changes, nothing remains."

That is certainly the way it seems in parish ministry today.

I took a leave of absence from the United Methodist Church in 1990 and returned to full time ministry in the United Church of Christ in 1999. When I left, if I had called parishioners who wanted me to leave and were actively working to accomplish that end, and said "I'm your pastor, and I need to see you," they would have found time to see me. When I returned to ministry nine years later, when I called to see parishioners that were encouraging supporters and said, "I'm your pastor, and I need to see you," they said "Can it wait until Sunday? Can we take care of it over the phone? Do you really need to see me?" Now when I call, I get answering machines and they rarely a return my phone call.

Everything changes, nothing remains. Hebrews 13:8 says, "Jesus Christ, the same yesterday, today and forever." It seems Jesus is the only thing that doesn't change!

I remember when, if you wanted a phone, you went to the phone company. They had exactly what you wanted: a black rotary desk phone that plugged into the wall. If you wanted privacy, you got a long cord and hid in the closet. I remember when the princess phone and the wall phone came out and colors became available. I remember being on a party line, listening to the ring to hear if it was for our house. Some people would quietly listen in on other people's conversations, so you had to be careful. I remember writing or typing – on a typewriter – letters, that I would mail through the post office and wait weeks for a reply.

If I asked dad what a word meant or how it was spelled, he would say, "Look it up!" I would look things up in the dictionary or the encyclopedia or at the public library. When I was a teen-ager, we had three sets of encyclopedias at home. I would randomly look up an article in one set and then compare it with the other two sets. I admit that makes me a geek! Now we just look it up on the internet.

The first cell phones in the 1970's were bricks that had two bags, one for the phone and one for the battery pack, and the phones held enough charge for half an hour of air time. In 1986, twenty-five percent of households had microwave ovens and thirty-six percent had personal computers. I remember making Jiffy-Pop on the stove. In November of 1989 the Berlin Wall came down and in October of 1990, East and West Germany reunited. In 1991 the Union of Soviet Socialist Republics collapsed into Russia and other republics. In 1994 Czechoslovakia split into the Czech Republic and Slovakia. When Senator McCain referred to Czechoslovakia in the 2008 presidential campaign, people wondered, "Who is this grandpa?"

At my high school graduation our speaker warned that the total amount of all available human knowledge was doubling every ten years. When I graduated from college four years later knowledge was doubling every five years. When I finished graduate school six years later it was every two years. Now all available human knowledge is doubling every six months. There is no way to keep up!

All of this cultural change has also led to change in the congregation. When I graduated college in 1973, my employer encouraged me to join a civic organization and to get active in a church. When I took my leave of absence from parish ministry and returned to secular employment in 1990, my employer did not ask or care about civic clubs or congregations, only the corporate bottom line: "What have you done for me lately?" was a frequent question.

In the 1950's everybody went to church; it was good for business. Today, maybe twenty-five percent of the adult population is in a corporate worship service of any faith during any given seven day period. Polls will say as many as a third respond that they were in a worship service in the current week, but most pollsters believe as many as half of them may be misstating the truth. Whether Protestant, Catholic, Orthodox, Jewish, Muslim, Buddhist or Hindu, most people would have to say in all honesty, "None of the above."

A number of our young adults consider themselves spiritual but not religious. We have generations who are unchurched: children whose grandparents chose not to participate in a religious community. One pastor shared with me an experience he had counseling a couple before their wedding. The bride to be grew up in that church and he had confirmed her in the faith. They went into the sanctuary to walk through the ceremony. The groom was agog. He asked, "What do you people do in this room?"

I've reminisced with my father about the changes he's seen in his life and in his ministry. He got his first loan when he moved from a church that paid him on the first of the month to a church that paid him on the last of the month. Nearly two months was a long time to go for a father with a growing family. He went to a bank and borrowed enough money to feed us for two months: twenty dollars. He got his first credit card when my younger sister took her first year of college in England, in 1971 when he was approaching 50.

When he started his ministry Dad lived in a small Indiana town. He would be awakened every morning by his neighbor, the town physician, starting his Model T Ford to begin making his daily house calls. Nothing in town would be scheduled Sunday morning or Wednesday evening: those were holy times for church functions. When Dad had to call members about a meeting, he would give the list of names to the local switchboard operator, who was a member of a different church, and she would call his committee members. When the school board hired a new superintendent, they didn't only tell him he had to join a church, they told him which church he had to join.

Times have changed!

Doctors no longer make house calls, though pastors are expected to. No physician is going to drive a twenty year old car unless it is a collectible classic that has been restored. Nobody reserves either Wednesday evening or Sunday morning for church. In Illinois, they do make the liquor stores wait until 10:00 to open on Sunday. There haven't been switchboard operators for some time; now meeting notices go out as an email blast. No employer tells workers where to go to church; most don't care if they go, and they won't give time off for workers to go.

Churches are no longer community centers, and Pastors are no longer community leaders. Attending worship is simply one thing among many on our Sunday morning "to do" lists. As churches and pastors have become less influential, pastors experience a rise in self-esteem issues. If we take our faith seriously, it is the most important fact in our lives; how can it be so unimportant to others? Everything changes, nothing remains!

Change is always stressful. Even when the change is positive and desirable, it creates stress. Much of the cultural change we are experiencing is not of our choosing; we are forced to adapt, whether we want to or not. Some of the change is painful, some of it frightening, and we cannot see the end of it. Frequent or continual change builds stress upon stress. Our congregations are often the only safe places where we can vent our frustration and release our pent up anxiety. Even the healthiest congregation needs to deal with conflict arising from this underlying stress and anxiety.

MEDITATION

Remember the world you grew up in. Did you watch television? Was it black and white or color? Did you listen to the radio? Was it AM or FM? Were you in a small town, big city, or open country? What were the different churches in your community? What different ethnic groups did you experience? What appliances were in the kitchen? How does all this compare with today?

QUESTIONS FOR REFLECTION AND CONVERSATION

1. How has the world changed in your lifetime? How was the world of your children different from the world you grew up in? How has it changed since?

2. What were the big events while you were growing up? How did you experience the news of the world?

3. What do you miss about the world you grew up in? What changes have been a benefit and which would you count as a loss?

4. How has your spiritual life developed from childhood, through youth, to adulthood? What changes in your spirituality do you notice?

4

It's Bigger than All of Us

I remember seeing images of the 2004 earthquake and tsunami in the Indian Ocean and the 2011 earthquake and tsunami in Japan. They were absolutely devastating: huge rolling mountains of waves, washing trains out to sea and destroying all evidence of human habitation.

The greatest truth of our time is not good news. The truth is that the changes that are upon us are greater than any of us can imagine them to be. We cannot fathom the height and depth and length and breadth of the changes we are currently living through. We're enduring a paradigm shift of epic proportion.

A paradigm is a model or pattern. In cultural terms, it's a set of expectations based upon prior experience. Our difficulty is that our previous experiences haven't adequately prepared us for the extent of change we're currently experiencing, and it's unreasonable to expect them to.

We who grew up when everyone went to church, when manufacturing drove our economy, when we believed that we could solve anything if given the right tools, and when the going got tough, the tough went shopping, are now living in a post-Christian, post-Modern, post-Industrial and post-Consumer age. Everything we learned growing up is out of date; nothing we once knew is valid any longer. We look at the world around us and it does not fit any model or pattern we have. The world is not what it once was, nor is it yet what it is going to be!

For the first time in fifteen hundred years, we have generations who are unchurched. We have grand-children whose grand-parents did not grow up going to church. Our communities have mosques and synagogues and temples. Our children have friends from families that are Muslim or Jewish, Buddhist or Hindu, Wicca or atheist.

The Modernist mind set believed we could solve any problem if we had enough information. Now we have information overload; there is so much information that no one can absorb it all and our problems just seem to get worse. No amount of information is going to solve them. We used to believe there was an objective reality, now everything seems to have some spin to it. We need to get our news from a wide variety of sources because each source has its own perspective and the truth is somewhere muddled in the middle.

Our Industrial society has become a service society, driven by the information age. Our country's greatest export the past decade or so has been all of our manufacturing jobs. We've entered a post-Industrial age.

We are even post-Consumerist. After 9/11 happened, President Bush urged us all to show our patriotism by going shopping. The great economic collapse was exacerbated in part by our giving up our shopping.

If we're not Christian, not Modern, not Industrial, not Consumerist, then what are we?

This still just touches the surface of the tsunami of change we are enduring.

Edwin Friedman in *A Failure of Nerve* describes a paradigm shift that has not been seen for five hundred years. Before 1500 roughly, most Europeans thought of the world as being flat, the earth as the center of the universe, all people being Catholic and nation-states as weak. If you wanted a copy of a document, it had to be handwritten. Bibles were kept chained in churches, and most people couldn't read them anyway. After the first few decades of the 1500s, Luther had split from Rome and translated the Bible into the language of the people. Gutenberg's printing press made copies of the scriptures available to the masses. The printing press in 1500 had the same cultural impact as the internet in our time: it made the mass transmission of information possible. Luther's protector was the Elector of Saxony, standing up as a secular leader against the Pope in Rome. Columbus had discovered what he called an entirely New World and Galileo and Copernicus warned us that we are not the center of anything. Everything that people believed to be true in 1470 was proven to be wrong by 1530. A generation had endured a paradigm shift that changed everything they thought to be so, not to be so. In the process of dealing with this massive cultural change, Europe also endured some terrible wars. A third of the German population died as a result.

With all the changes we are enduring, we haven't reached that level of violence, though we're not done yet.

Phyllis Tickle in *The Great Emergence* builds on this "once every 500 years" model for church history. In the fourth century, the first and second Nicene Councils decreed that all Christian must affirm a particular understanding of the Trinity and of the Incarnation, thus excluding some of the oldest churches in Christendom. The Nestorians, the Armenian Church, the Coptic church in Egypt; all the oldest churches in the Middle East were excluded. In the dividing, the church grew.

Around 1000 A.D. we had the Great Schism between the Western Catholic church and the Eastern Orthodox Church. Again, in the dividing, the church was renewed. Around 1500, Western Europe split between Catholic and Protestant. Again, in the dividing the church was renewed and re-energized. Now we have come to another 500 year interval and the church is experiencing another dividing and renewing cycle.

But the "once every 500 years" time frame may not be enough. Phillip Jenkins in The Next Christendom argues that church history can be divided into three millennia. The first thousand years the church was largely non-European. The second thousand years the church was largely European, either in geography or by the missionary zeal of Europeans. Now the church is again becoming non-European. The church is expanding exponentially south of the equator, in South America, Africa and Asia. Where the church is growing, it is also more conservative, more evangelical and more Pentecostal than in Europe and North America. He describes the first millennium as the age of the Father, the second as the age of the Son and the third that we are now entering as the age of the Spirit. He also says that Europe and North America will become increasingly irrelevant to global Christianity, which will be increasingly Pentecostal, charismatic, and conservative and tied to its ancient roots.

But even once every thousand years may not be a big enough time frame. Harvey Cox has said that the church is going through its greatest period of change and growth since the first century.

Whichever of these is closest to reality, the truth remains the same: none of us can imagine the level of change we are currently enduring. I am a human being, a mortal. The Bible gives me three score years to live, or perhaps three score and ten. Actuaries might give me 85 or 90. In any case, I can't imagine something that's measured on the scale of centuries. I don't have the experience to form that large a paradigm. So perhaps, if there's good news, it's that I'm not supposed to understand everything that is changing.

The cultural shift we're experiencing is of historic proportion. It creates stress and anxiety in us all. The congregation is a safe place to vent, verbally or behaviorally. Every time my Women's Guild meets, they begin by sharing their frustrations at how things have changed in their lives. My confirmation class, made up of thirteen year olds, can identify how radically things have changed in their lifetimes. Retired clergy share how lost they feel in the contemporary church, frequently adding that the church has changed so much, they could not enter the ministry in the current situation. Change creates stress, stress leads to conflict.

MEDITATION

Remember your first time at the seashore. How old were you? Was it summer or another season? Remember seeing the ocean for the first time. How vast did it seem? Remember the sound of the waves hitting the shore, the feel of the foam in your face. Remember the rolling of the waves.

Imagine playing in the waves, feeling them break over your head, push you to shore, pull you back out. What does it feel like having the waves wash over you? Being in over your head?

QUESTIONS FOR REFLECTION AND CONVERSATION

1. Reflect on the 2004 Indian Ocean tsunami and the 2011 Japanese earthquake. How did you react to the news? What responses did you or your congregation make? What impact have these events had on your life?

2. What do you think of the "five hundred year cycle" theory of paradigm shifts? How nearly do you think this model describes historical reality?

3. What do you remember of the cultural shifts that were happening at the time of the Protestant Reformation, the last "500 year shift"? How were things changing then? How does this knowledge help us relate to the cultural changes we are currently undergoing?

4. How have the cultural changes we've experienced affected your spirituality? How have you dealt with it?

5

CONGREGATIONAL CONSEQUENCES

We're living through an immense cultural shift that is beyond our ability to comprehend or measure, but the good news is that we are surviving. Change is always disruptive; this level of change borders on chaotic. Our society is changing radically and rapidly. Even though many resist the tide of change, our congregations are changing. The role of the church in society at large and our local communities has changed. The attitudes toward faith, church and clergy have changed. These are massive changes on a global level with a profound impact on our emotional health. The level of stress produced by these changes makes periodic conflicts inevitable.

Most congregations, regardless of theological differences, share two truths: 1. We don't much like change. 2. Our idea of ancient history is "when I was your age." Change is disruptive; it disturbs the way things are. We like things the way they are, the way they used to be, the way God intended them to forever be. Churches are intrinsically conservative organizations. Whatever their theology or their politics, most congregations are inherently conservative cultures: they don't like change!

We've heard the "seven last words of the church." "We have always done it this way." Or "We have never done that here before." We don't care; we're still not changing! The most important tradition in most congregations is whatever we've done the past five or ten years. The most politically or theologically liberal or progressive congregation remains sociologically conservative. It's our nature to seek and maintain homeostasis. We seek stability rather than balance. Stability is best attained by staying put. Balance is necessary when we're in motion. Coping with change requires balance, not stability.

Even if we can preserve the past within the congregation, the world around us is changing in ways beyond our understanding, much less our control. Even if our congregational life is relatively healthy, we still have to live within the greater world. We end up with SAD congregations: Stessed, Anxious and Dysfunctional. Change, even when it is good, healthy and desirable, produces stress. We must adjust to the change, find balance rather than stability. Repeated changes, change that becomes constant, can only build anxiety if we seek stability rather than balance. We live in an anxious age. People and organizations that are stressed and anxious have an increasingly difficult time functioning in a healthy pattern. A healthy pattern calls for balance. When we're stressed and anxious, we become dysfunctional. With the level and pace of change we are going through, we're very stressed and anxious. Our churches become SAD congregations: Stressed, Anxious and Dysfunctional.

Niels Bohr in describing quantum theory wrote, "Anyone who isn't shocked by quantum theory has not understood it." Anyone who isn't shocked by the scope of cultural change we are going through doesn't understand it. It may not be healthy for our congregations to be SAD, but given our cultural realities, it is normal.

Quantum theory describes the universe as composed of subatomic particles of energy vibrating in harmony with one another in such a way that they create the physical world we see. The universe seeks balance rather than stability.

SAD congregations will have conflict. The presenting events of the conflict will be the systemic issues that the congregation does not know how to deal with, doesn't want to deal with and may not be able to recognize or acknowledge. The tremendous changes buffeting our society infect our congregations when we bring our own stress and anxiety with us. In the relatively safe and protected atmosphere of the church, we tend to act out our stress and anxiety in ways that are dysfunctional. In ways analogous to the Thirty Year

War that devastated Germany during the 1500's it seems as if the church is in the midst of thirty years of internecine guerilla warfare in our local congregations in the name of the gospel. "Guerrilla" is the Spanish phrase for "little war." Many of our congregations unconsciously engage in guerilla warfare, little wars that consist of petty behavior: gossip, triangulation, sniping, sarcasm (literally "biting the cheek"), and occasionally flare up into more hostile and dysfunctional behavior that can result in dismissed staff, lost members, divided or closed congregations.

We have unintentionally become the church described by David Kinnaman in boldly titled book, *UnChristian*. We focus on rules and regulations rather than relationships; on doctrine and dogma rather than the divine drama unfolding before us. We are seen as out of touch with the new realities and stuck on the past, as being hypocritical, judgmental, sexually repressed and over-driven by political issues. "Only a small percentage of outsiders strongly believe that the labels 'respect, love, hope, and trust' describe Christianity." A SAD congregation, one that is Stressed, Anxious and Dysfunctional, won't effectively embody or communicate the gospel. If we can focus our congregational energy on seeking balance rather than stability, we can become congregations that are GLAD instead of SAD: Good, Loving and Dynamic!

MEDITATION

Earlier we focused on our first congregational crisis from our perspective. Now look back on that experience from the congregation's perspective. What events precipitated the crisis? What attitudes made it inevitable? How did the congregation react to the events? What feelings were current during the crisis? How did they survive? What resources proved helpful to them?

Seeing from the other person's perspective can help us find a third way, a way through the crisis that neither of us would find from our own perspective.

QUESTIONS FOR REFLECTION AND CONVERSATION

1. How does your congregation deal with change? Identify specific examples and instances.

2. What do you think of the "Stressed – Anxious – Dysfunctional" model? How does it fit the congregations you have served? Again, identify specific examples and instances. Can you see a way to become GLAD: Good, Loving And Dynamic?

3. We've all heard of the "seven last words of the church." Have you been in a situation where death of an organization or a congregation was preferable to change? If so, describe that experience.

4. How have you been able to find a sense of balance in your spiritual life? Do you sense a distinction between balance and stability?

6

IMPROVING OUR IMMUNITIES

Studies indicate that children raised in the city develop more allergies and sensitivities than do children raised in the country. The supposition is that country kids spend more time outside and exposed to more allergens, germs, bacteria and viruses. Because of this exposure, their bodies develop stronger immune systems so they are better able to fend off attacks as adults.

There are a number of conditions that attack the human immune system. HIV / Aids may be the first to come to mind, but diabetes, arthritis, multiple sclerosis, celiac disease and hepatitis are all on the list of conditions that stress our immune system and weaken it, some even cause our immune system to attack our body. What often happens in these cases is that an opportunistic disease attacks our bodies and our weakened immune system can't fend it off. Victims of immune system conditions frequently die, not from the condition itself, but from the opportunistic diseases that our weakened system can't defend against.

Physicians know that long term stress weakens the body's immune system, making it more susceptible to opportunistic infections. The church's body suffers the same consequences from long term stress. We get tired, weary, weakened; it becomes harder for us to keep our defenses up, to maintain our vigilance. We need Specific, Practical, Actionable Methods to prevent our becoming stressed, anxious and dysfunctional; some positive SPAM to prevent our becoming SAD.

The world is not what it once was, what any of us remember. The change is not done; if anything, it's increasing both in speed

and in scope. The rate and range of this cultural shift is beyond our
limited human ability to measure or understand. Transition always
creates tension: change causes stress, even when we want the change
and especially when we don't. We are going to continue living in
this radically changing world. As individuals, we will be constantly
exposed to these stress-causing transitions. As parishioners, we will
continue to bring this stress into our congregations. None of this is
going to change it will not go away and we cannot lessen its force.
What we can do is improve our defenses. We need to strengthen
our immune system. We don't want our congregations to be SAD
– stressed, anxious and dysfunctional!

Here are disciplines we can put into place in our congregations
that will help us inoculate ourselves from these opportunistic infections. Here are specific, practical, actionable methods to vaccinate
ourselves from becoming stressed, anxious and dysfunctional.

1. Always talk about everything. Anytime there is something
you think that you can't talk about, there are two problems. First
there's the issue that seems to be unmentionable, which is the
lesser problem. Second, there's the fact that you think it can't be
discussed, which is the greater problem. Silence is rarely golden!
Communication is the tie that binds us in our relationships, that
keeps us relating. We need to be able to talk about any issue, no
matter how awkward or embarrassed we may be in discussing it.

2. Direct and face to face: never triangulate! "Triangulation"
occurs when I have an issue with you and I go to somebody else
about it instead of going straight to you and our discussing this face
to face and person to person. Congregations have a subconscious
tendency to triangulate and it's never healthy. Again, we may feel
embarrassed; it might be awkward, but always talk face to face,
never behind the back.

3. Transparency and Confidentiality. Silence isn't golden and
secrets aren't good. Information needs to be available. At the same
time, not everybody needs to know everything. Confidentiality
means that those who need to know, know what they need to know

when they need to know it. It is means that information needs to be made available and will be available, as it is appropriate. No secret meetings, no hidden agendas, no under the table negotiations, no behind the back shenanigans. We are honest and direct, handling our affairs with mutual trust and respect, and maintaining confidentiality and transparency in all our discussions and decisions.

4. Love one another – no matter what! Love is the first and greatest commandment, "love God with all your heart, soul, mind and strength," the second commandment that makes the first one tangible, "love your neighbor as you love yourself," the new commandment, "love one another," the first fruit of the Spirit in Galatians 5:22-23, the greatest gift of the Spirit in 1 Corinthians 13, and fulfills the Law in Romans 13:10. 1 John 4:12 tells us "as we love one another, God's love is made complete." Love God, love our neighbor, love ourselves, love one another, and even love our enemies! If we don't get anything else right, we've got to get this right. Nothing else is more emphasized in the New Testament.

The early Christians were ridiculed for their beliefs, persecuted by the Romans, scorned by the Jews, dismissed by the Greeks. But the pagan philosophers were silenced by the hospitality and charity demonstrated by the early church. All they could say was, "My, how these Christians love one another!" Acts of love may yet prove to be the greatest evangelism tool we have.

5. Listen twice, speak once. We have two ears and one mouth; maybe there's a reason for this. Nobody ever learned anything by speaking, only by listening. Psalm 62:11-12 records, "Once God has spoken it, twice have I heard: power belongs to God, and steadfast love as well." We're more likely to learn if we ask questions and listen well before we speak up. We're also less likely to upset others.

6. Say please and thank you. Sometimes it's easier to be polite with strangers than with friends or family. Remembering our manners can help smooth rocky times. Asking others rather than telling them, offering help whenever possible, expressing gratitude are all simple yet important elements. An attitude of gratitude has been called the foundation of a faithful life.

7. Do what you say and say what you do. Nobody likes a hypocrite; it's important that our words and our deeds match. If we say we will do something, we need to do it. Holding ourselves to our word is an important element of covenant building and building trusting relationships.

One of the running arguments I'd had with our previous Church Council was their not following our Constitution and By-laws. I said we needed to do what it says or change what it says to accurately describe what we do. Our words and our deeds needed to match; say what we do and do what we say.

8. Behavioral Covenants and Five fingers. Many organizations adopt behavioral covenants. As clergy, we are accountable to a Code of Ethics and take Boundary training that serve as behavioral covenants. I've seen Behavioral Covenants that were a few pages long. My problem with all of these is that, when we get hot under the collar, we aren't likely to review the behavioral covenants that may apply in that situation. They're too long to be practical.

I found a behavioral covenant that works for me, that is easy to remember and simple to apply: the five fingers of faithful fellowship. We can look at our hand, whether it's open and receptive to give or receive, ready to be offered in friendship, willing to shake with another or even clenched in a fist. We've got five fingers: 1) love one another, 2) welcome one another, 3) encourage one another, 4) pray for one another, 5) do all this non-judgmentally (our opposable thumb, touching all the others).

We've used a Shaker greeting from time to time as part of our Passing of the Peace or Greeting One Another in our Sunday worship services: "The Christ in me greets the Christ in thee and draws us together in love." When we approach the other person open to the Christ that is within them and wanting to share the Christ that is in us, we are drawn together in love.

This is like the "Namaste" greeting shared by Hindus. I've heard it translated to mean "The best and greatest within me greets the best and greatest within thee." That is a good way to begin any conversation.

These are all specific, practical, actionable methods to help strengthen our congregation's immune system against any opportunistic stressed, anxious dysfunctional attacks.

MEDITATION

Remember the last time you have the flu or a cold. How did your body feel? What preventive measures do you now take to keep your body well?

QUESTIONS FOR REFLECTION AND DISCUSSION

1. What practices do you have in place to help keep your congregation healthy?

2. What is your reaction to the specific, practical, actionable methods to prevent our becoming stressed, anxious and dysfunctional?

3. How is your congregation's immune system? How can you do a check-up of your congregational health?

4. How is your personal immune system? What ideas from this chapter can you adapt to strengthen it?

7

PREPARING FOR POST TIME

When the trainer is getting the horse ready for race day, preparing to enter the starting gate, they are getting ready for post-time. The trainer walks the horse around the paddock, allowing the horse to gently exercise and loosen its muscles. The trainer maintains a strong hold and a short rein, not wanting the horse to get overly excited or easily distracted. The trainer helps the horse focus on the race ahead. Our congregations are like a horse, preparing to run the race set before it, and we need to be like that trainer, helping the horse focus.

We live in a "Post" world: post-modern, post-industrial, post-consumerist, post-Christendom. With everything that is behind us, how do we cope in this new and different "post" culture?

Paul reminds us in what is my favorite passage in all scripture, "This one thing I do: forgetting what lies behind and straining forward to what lies ahead, I press on toward the goal for the prize of the upward call of God that is ours in Christ Jesus" (Philippians 3:13-14). Just a few verses previously, Paul had listed all the things he had to boast in, all his heritage he had to be proud of "circumcised on the eighth day, of the nation of Israel, of the tribe of Benjamin, a Hebrew of Hebrews, as to the Law a Pharisee, as to zeal a persecutor of the church, as to righteousness in the Law, blameless"(Philippians 3:5-6). No brag, just fact. Yet he counted all he had to boast in to be refuse, garbage, less than nothing, for the sake of the Gospel. No matter how magnificent our heritage, what lies behind us is less than what lies before us.

Immediately after reminding Israel of God's mighty acts in creation and in their liberation from Egypt through the sea, God says in Isaiah 43: 18-19, "Do not remember the former things or consider the things of old. I am about to do a new thing; now it spring forth, do you not perceive it?" God encourages Israel, saying that the Exodus that gave birth to their nation and even the act of creation itself pale before what God has yet to do.

After all, "if anyone is in Christ, all creation is made new. Everything old has passed away and all things are made new" (2 Corinthians 5:17). The radicalness of this verse says not only "if one person is in Christ, that person is made new" but "if only one person is in Christ, all creation is made new!" What is more, it's written as an accomplished fact. This gives new meaning to the Three Musketeer's motto, "All for one and one for all!"

The world has grown more secular, our communities more diverse and our parishes less parochial. We're more aware of the larger world, which is a good thing. Sometimes, with this growing awareness and increasing attraction, we forget who we are as a church. Attraction becomes distraction. The race horse wears blinders so that it can focus on the path ahead; the rider and the trainer keep a tight rein to better harness the horse's energy. Having a mission or vision statement that clearly and succinctly declares our self-identity helps strengthen the membrane of the wall between our congregation and the greater community, as in any healthy cell. The wall needs to be permeable to provide access and awareness. It also needs to be present; we need to know who we are, what we are about, and what we are not.

A mission statement needs to be clearly focused, easily understood and strike at the core of the organization, words that are uniquely descriptive. I have shared in one-day workshops with congregations that help them write a statement that is understood and that underscores their self-identity.

At St. Peter's, we started with our purpose as stated in our constitution: "the purpose of this church shall be to worship God, to preach the gospel of Jesus Christ, and to celebrate the Sacraments;

to realize Christian fellowship and unity within this church and the Church Universal; to render loving service toward humankind; and to strive for righteousness, justice and peace." It's certainly descriptive, but hardly unique, and too long.

We moved to "a generationally diverse congregation that engages members with a variety of programs designed to meet the specific spiritual and social needs of individuals and groups" and shortened it to "St. Peter's is committed to providing a firm, spiritual foundation for the future of Frankfort."

We had good response to some shorter slogans: "The historic church for the village of Frankfort." "Cherishing our past, celebrating our present, creating our future." "Building Community through worship, service and growth." "Classic worship with the timeless message of our eternal Savior." "Serious Christians with a sense of humor." "The church with the chimes; a church for the times." (We have a carillon that plays at noon and at 6:00 pm.)

Samples from some of our sister congregations: "We seek to embody and celebrate God's love by being a community that lives Christ's compassion and promotes justice, healing and wholeness of life; a joyous family where all are welcome to join together to grow in faith and love." "We are a family of faith that seeks to walk in the footsteps of Christ and to know God's will and purpose in our lives. Our doors are open to all who wish to join our journey." "Seeking, Serving and Sharing Christ." "Open Theologically, Growing Spiritually, Concerned Socially." "Love God, Grow in the Holy Spirit, Serve with Christ."

Having a mission or purpose statement is critical to knowing who you are. It needs to be short enough so that it can be easily remembered and plain enough so that it can be easily understood by non-members. The experience of composing a mission statement can be energizing and encouraging for a congregation.

Some congregations match every proposed program or event against their mission statement. If it fits, they'll do it; if it doesn't match up, they won't do the program no matter how appealing it might be, because it's not what they're about.

At one time, members were required to memorize a congregational statement of faith, which was repeated in unison regularly in the worship services. They can still recite that and mark this as an important memory in their faith journey. It not only tells them who "we" are, it tells them who they are.

A clear sense of purpose, of mission, strengthens our core, it keeps us on track and on target and helps prevent our getting distracted. A sense of vision tells us where we are going. Developing and reviewing these statements give us a stronger sense of identity as a congregation.

A mission statement or purpose statement or vision statement can serve as the blinders and the tight rein serve for the race horse: it can help keep us focused on who we are and what we are about, firm on the foundation we have adopted ourselves to. The Alban Institute calls it "steady on purpose, flexible on strategy."

When my son was in the Marines, he was taught two principles that can be applied to our congregations. First, the unit always has two objectives: accomplish the mission and care for your comrades. They're kept and dealt with in that order: mission first, comrades second. Second, when encountering a hurdle or complication to accomplishing the mission, we adjust, adapt and overcome. If we have a clear sense of mission and understand that our personal preferences are secondary to our corporate cohesion, we can move as a body to adjust our tactics and adapt our strategies to overcome any obstacle. Or as the Alban Institute said, "steady on purpose, flexible on strategy."

It's Post time. Are we ready for the race?

MEDITATION

When have you been involved in athletic competition? How did you prepare: in the days ahead of the event, and on the day of the event?

QUESTIONS FOR REFLECTION AND DISCUSSION

1. The words "disciple" and "discipline" share a common root. A disciple is one who follows and discipline is how one follows. What examples from your daily routine can you call to mind that serve to demonstrate your Christian faith? How do you "walk the talk"?

2. Are the images of blinders and a tight rein on a race horse helpful in describing the church's need to stay focused? What other images come to mind?

3. Have there been occasions when you have undertaken a project or program that did not fit well with your mission and purpose? What were the consequences?

4. How does a sense of purpose and focus relate to your spiritual life? Do you have a personal mission statement? If so, how do you use it?

8

Running Hard Just to Keep Up

I was walking from the church to the parsonage with my youngest son, Joshua, in tow. Joshua was a pre-schooler at the time. I'd learned to walk with my father, who has a very brisk pace. As I walked, I kept tugging on Joshua's arm. After a few tugs encouraging him to keep up, he confessed, "Daddy, I'm running as fast as I can!"

That woke me out of myself and I realized the truth of it. I was walking with my normal stride and pace. Joshua was a fraction of my size and his legs much smaller than mine. What for me was a brisk, business-like pace for me was for him flying low near the ground. I did slow my pace.

There are a number of things we can do to strengthen ourselves as clergy and as congregations living in a world of conflict and change. There is an innumerable amount of things we have to do on a daily basis just to survive. Pastors are generalists who must juggle priorities and perform multiple tasks simultaneously, learning to do all things well. We have "to do" lists that are never done. We run hard just to keep up!

Just because we can survive does not mean it will be easy. We can survive in the midst of conflict and change; we can survive as a people of faith in an increasingly secular society. It will be worth it, but it won't be easy. We get up, we get at it, and we get going. We are little Joshua, running hard to keep up, living in a world that tugs at us to catch up.

Our calling as Christians, as congregations and as pastors isn't intended to be easy. If it was easy, anyone could do it. It's intended to be worthy, worth the effort. The call of scripture is to live a life worthy of the Gospel.

Writing in the fourth century, John Chrysostom observes that there are some things that we wonder at, yet without fear: artistic beauty, the wonder of nature. There are also those things that we wonder at with fear: standing at a precipice, or the depths of the ocean. For us, the high dive for the first time, or the glass-bottomed observation deck of the Willis Tower (formerly Sears). We get dizzy and recoil with fear.

We can, with John, choose to respond with faith rather than with fear, acknowledging that things are amazing and marvelous and sometimes beyond us to understand, we cannot attain them. With Joshua, we can also confess that we are running as fast as we can, and trust that the one holding our hand will keep us secure, even when we can't figure out how.

Early in my career I complained to my mentor that, no matter how hard I worked, no matter how many hours I put in, I simply could not get everything done. I was in over my head and not up to the task. It was too much for me and I was overwhelmed. Instead of giving me pity or sage advice, he laughed.

David, you will never be able to get everything done. It's not possible. So just do what you want to do and don't worry about the rest!

I thought that was terrible advice. I had a lot to do. All of it was important. And besides, I was the only one who could do it! It would be incredibly selfish of me to just do what I wanted.

You can't do the impossible. If you try to do it all, you'll get exhausted, burn yourself out and not be any good to anyone. If you focus on doing what everybody else thinks you should do, you will get frustrated, burn yourself out and not be any good to anyone. If you do what you love, it will feed and strengthen you, and you will enjoy your ministry and stay with it for the long haul. That will be good for everyone. And all that other stuff, if it is important, they'll find a way to get it done, and that will be good for them.

The bad news is that none of us can do it all. The good news is that if we do what we love, it will feed us and we can keep on keeping on!

MEDITATION

Remember standing on the high dive the first time, waiting to take that plunge into the pool. How high up were you? How high did it seem? Did you think of climbing back down? What encouraged you to take that leap? How hard is it to simply "let go"?

QUESTIONS FOR REFLECTION AND DISCUSSION

1. When did you feel in over your head, overwhelmed by priorities and concerns: too much to do and too little time to do it in? How did you choose what to do? How do you prioritize your time?

2. What do you most enjoy in your ministry? How does it energize you? How can you find ways to spend more time doing what you love?

3. Who has been a mentor for you spiritually? How have they guided you in your ministry?

9

FAITH OUT OF FOCUS

The pace of life has picked up the past few decades; we all have more going on. The church is less at the center of our community life and more at the edge. In an increasingly secular society, the sacred becomes less central. There are always "other things to do"! We suffer sometimes from information overload. It's no wonder things get out of focus.

When we don't have a clear sense of purpose, a clear sense of mission and a clear sense of vision - who we are and where we are going — it's easy for us to get distracted. As Yogi Berra once said, "If you don't know where you are going, it doesn't matter how you get there."

When a congregation isn't solidly grounded in a common purpose, doesn't identify a common sense of mission and doesn't see a united and focused vision, it will get distracted with personal issues. We've all experienced congregations when parish politics and congregational cliques are at play. Parish politics aren't inherently wrong; politics is simply a description of how decisions are made and actions taken. When we lose our common mission and focus, our decision making process can become blurred.

Every congregation has small groups. This is how we relate with others who share a common interest and how we relate with others within the congregation. Small groups are a vital part of healthy congregational life. Yet, when a congregation loses its shared vision and common purpose, small groups intended to facilitate mission and fellowship can become power centers and function as cliques, each pushing its own agenda over the agenda of the whole. When our attachment is to the small group or our opinions and preferences, we cloud the issue and confuse the process. Ego comes into play.

A member of St. Peter's described ego as "edging God out" (thank you Susan Lynch). That's what we do.

We're like Peter in the boat during that midnight storm. He sees Jesus approaching, walking on the water, and Jesus invites Peter to come out of the boat. Peter does, and surprisingly walks on the water also. Until he takes his eyes off Jesus and focuses instead on the storm raging around him; then he begins to sink, and Jesus has to raise him up.

When we take our eyes off Jesus, we see only the storm and lose our focus. We focus instead on ourselves, our egos, and we edge God out. As Christians, we're called to live out the life of Christ. As congregations, we're the body of Christ. As Paul writes, Christ is our head.

To say that Christ is our head means that Christ is master, lord, savior, mentor, leader, teacher, role model, and example. Christ is not only God's revelation of who God is; Christ is God's demonstration of what God means for us to be. The supremacy of Christ in Colossians 1:15-20 is balanced with the humility of Christ in Philippians 2:1-13, so that the headship of Christ is a spiritual authority.

Likewise, pastors can offer themselves as role models, examples of what it means for us in our time and place to be incarnations of the one who is the incarnation of God. The role of the pastor is more important than is the function: how we fulfill the duties of the pastoral office is more important than is the particular duties themselves. For good or for ill, congregations look to their pastors for this spiritual leadership, offering up an example of "this is what it means to be Christian." Most jobs have a "to do" list. Ministry has a "to be" list. Not everyone can accept this, which is why not everyone is called. Being a pastor is more than doing a job. It's even more than "doing ministry."

Parson may be an archaic title, but it's accurate. A parson is a person grounded in Christ. Our authority must be grounded in our spirituality if it is to be authentic.

Part of the problem we experienced at St. Peter's in 2007 was tension over the question of who is in charge. Congregational structure plays a role in this. In a hierarchical system, the lines of authority are clearly drawn. My father shared about a time when a church he was serving was having conflict over the question of who was in charge. As a Methodist, he called in his District Superintendent, who opened the Book of Discipline and read, "The pastor is in charge." He closed the book and asked, "Are there any questions?" It was a short meeting! In a congregational system it's not that simple; there are no outside authorities to call in. The congregation is autonomous.

We had conflict between the Church Council and the congregation. The Council thought it was in charge, while the congregation believed the congregation as a whole, meeting in session, had final authority. It became a question of "who wants what" rather than a discernment process seeking to know and do Christ's will. We'd edged God out.

Christ is the head, we are the body. We're not called to the church to do what we want or what the pastor wants or what the Council wants; we're called to do what Christ wants.

A verse I often repeat is Psalm 115:1, "Not to us, O Lord, not ever to us, but to you be glory and to you be praise, for your steadfast love toward us and your abiding faithfulness." Even Jesus in the garden of Gethsemane, praying for his cup to pass and life to be spared, ended, "Nevertheless, not my will but thine be done."

"Getting our own way" can never be a motivation for us, as individual members or pastors, as small groups or as the congregation as a whole. The ego has no place in church.

I believe the ego to serve us psychologically, even as the appendix serves our digestive systems. While it's of little practical necessity today, evolutionary biologists speculate that the appendix once was necessary to aid in our digestion, when our diets consisted of much more roughage and raw foods. It was necessary when we were primitive, but it's not needed today.

Our ego is a gift of God, and as such a good thing. We all need our egos when we are infants; we need to let others know of our needs: when we're hungry or thirsty or wet or hurt. Our world naturally centers on us.

We've grown, and hopefully matured. Our world no longer centers on ourselves. Other people are not just objects for us to use. We value their relationships, their place in our lives and therefore their wants, needs, opinions and aspirations. Our ego no longer needs to be constantly attended to; it has become an emotional appendix.

We need to be in balance: maintaining a strong positive self-image that affirms who we are as children of God without asserting our wills over others. We can affirm ourselves without becoming aggressive toward others. When I see "the Christ in me," I see myself as a child of God and a gift of God. When I see "the Christ in thee," I see you as my brother or sister in Christ and likewise a gift of God.

When our faith gets out of focus, we tend to focus instead on ourselves. This will always lead to conflict, as we each have counter-balancing egos. The corrective is to keep a steady focus on Christ as our head, on "outdoing one another in affection," "counting others greater than yourselves," and remembering to love our neighbor as – "equal to" our love for ourselves.

MEDITATION

Imagine a little infant. See how small and helpless it is. Observe how it communicates and what its priorities and concerns are, how its entire being is focused on itself.

Now imagine life as an adult. Imagine an adult behaving the same way a small infant does, with the same priorities and concerns. Remember Paul in 1 Corinthians 13: "When I was a child, I acted like a child; I reasoned like a child, I behaved like a child. When I became an adult, I put away my childish ways."

QUESTIONS FOR REFLECTION AND DISCUSSION

1. Remember a time recently that you caught yourself behaving childishly, when you found yourself wanting your own way simply because it was your way. What triggered that behavior? How did your behavior change when you became aware of it? What was the outcome of that event? How might it have been different?

2. What is an instance when you affirmed your own power? Were you able to also affirm the power of others? How have you helped others claim their power? When was there a time that personal power was mismanaged? How did people's behavior change? What were the triggers then? What was the outcome? How did you handle that situation, and how might you have handled it differently?

3. Can you share some times that your ego has edged God out?

10

A Hospital along the Way

The church has been described in a great many ways: body of Christ, a colony of heaven, God's proving ground, fellowship of believers, and family of faith. The early church described itself as a court of law, where we confessed our guilt and depended upon God's mercy. The Greek mystics saw themselves as an academy for divine wisdom.

The church as family fits most of our experiences. It's always safe to behave as though everyone is related to everyone else. Thousands of congregations are exactly that: a place where one extended family gathers to worship, with a few of their friends.

The model of the church as court room suited the theological development of the western church. We were sinners and Christ was the cure. The person who felt convicted came, presented himself or herself before the judge in a court, confessed their sin, submitted to the penance that was due, accepted a sentence that was then suspended pending their changed lives. Christ was our defense attorney and the Holy Spirit our comforter before God the righteous judge.

The model from the eastern church of the church as an academy of learning, where one engaged in the pursuit of holy wisdom, was less judgmental. The church is the place where the ignorant can be educated; we are not criminals to be judged but students to be educated. Many denominations and most congregations still pride themselves on their educational ministries.

Another model from the early Eastern church is that of hospital: the church is the place where the wounded come to be healed, where the broken come to be made whole, where the infirm come to be strengthened. Jesus was noted for his healing miracles. The church has always maintained hospitals and a healing ministry. When Rome was devastated with a plague and people abandoned loved ones who were diseased for fear of catching the disease, the church in Rome cared for those who were infected, even at risk to their own lives.

Our society today suffers from the sickness of stress, the contagion of conflict, a pestilence of loneliness. The stress caused by change is not going away and will not lessen. Our congregations can be places where those who are infected with the stress caused by the level of change and the resulting symptoms of conflict can come for recuperation and rehabilitation. We can be a place of rest along the way, where the travelers of this world can find refreshment from their journey.

The truth is that most of us are walking wounded. Psychologists estimate that seventy-five percent of us have some kind of issue that we're working on or that is working on us; we have some problem that would be helped by having someone who cares to talk it over with. Not a major psychosis, just something troubling us. We need someone who cares, who will listen to us and be a sounding board for us. In a healthy, healing congregation, we take turns being the patient and being the caregiver.

A hospital maintains an emergency room, where people with critical problems can find immediate care, diagnostic services to help people grow in their self-understanding, birthing rooms where new life can be nurtured and convalescent wings where people are allowed to recover and strengthen so that they may once again enter the larger world, refreshed and revived. Therapy is available to help people better cope with their daily lives after their release from the hospital.

I suggest that the ideal hospital serves as a better model for our congregations today than does that of the courtroom or classroom. The model can include fitness centers as well. There has been a growth in the number of centers for physical fitness and people available as personal trainers for physical fitness. The church can be a center for spiritual fitness, with teachers, counselors and pastors who can serve as personal coaches for that spiritual fitness.

MEDITATION

Remember a time you were sick, even hospitalized. Remember the physical aches and pains, and also remember the emotional longing, the need to have someone who simply cares. Likewise, remember caring for a loved one who was sick, how the physical act of caring was an expression of the emotional relationship and bond that was shared.

QUESTIONS FOR REFLECTION AND CONVERSATION

1. Brainstorm each on how the church is like a courtroom, a classroom and a hospital room. How do you assess each analogy?

2. What would change in your congregation if you were to implement the model of the church as hospital?

3. What is your response to the link between physical fitness and spiritual fitness? How can this be a helpful model for your congregation?

11

KNOWING WHEN TO SAY WHEN

There is a line in "The Gambler," a song by Kenny Rogers, that goes, "You've got to know when to hold 'em, know when to fold 'em, know when to walk away and know when to run." This book is about caring for and staying with churches in conflict. This author also knows that there comes a time when we must move on. We've got to know when to hold them and when to fold them.

We all have limits beyond which we simply cannot go. Will and desire have nothing to do with it; it's not a matter of perseverance or determination. I can only run so fast, or type so fast. It's not about trying harder or wanting it more. We're finite creatures. Part of our being mortal creatures is that we will die; we're limited in time and space.

There is a scene in Monty Python's "Meaning of Life" that takes place in a restaurant. A particularly large gentleman consumes an inordinate amount of food; he is near bursting. The waiter offers him a mint as dessert, "It is wafer thin." He reluctantly swallows it and immediately explodes. It's a funny scene in the Monty Python tradition, and it illustrates a point: how do we know when to say when? How do we determine how much is enough and how much we can tolerate?

There have been plenty of times someone else was filling my cup, asking me to "Say 'when'!" I need to know when to say when, when enough is enough.

I spent most of my life in the United Methodist Church, where pastors serve under the appointment of a District Superintendent. Each year I was asked a multiple choice question: 1) I must move.

2) I prefer moving. 3) I am indifferent. 4) I prefer staying. 5) I strongly prefer staying. In the itinerant system, clergy are always "available" for appointment, but personal, family or parish concerns may influence one's preferences. While I was asked each year what I preferred, I was never asked to justify or explain my preferences. Again, how does one decide when it is time to move on, when enough is enough?

The United Church of Christ is a congregational system, where pastors and parishes seek out one another. Every Wednesday, the national office of the United Church of Christ publishes a listing of congregations currently seeking pastoral profiles for consideration. A profile is roughly equivalent to a resume, except it is twenty pages long instead of one or two. I can have my profile sent to anyone anywhere and they can all pitch them in the round file. It is the opposite of the appointment process, but begs the same question: how do you know when it's time?

We call the process discernment, but realistically it's as much about exhaustion or frustration with where one is at and even the ego's desire for some church that's bigger and better, healthier, that has no problems. Reality is that there's no such place. As Erma Bombeck said, "The grass is always greener over the septic tank."

The times I have moved it has always been out of wanderlust; "itchy feet" I call it. There was boredom with the same old routine, curiosity about being someplace else and facing different challenges and opportunities. I've never faced the dilemma of needing to move out of necessity, because I couldn't stand the place where I was at or I was forced out by the congregation, the Council or some clique in the church. Almost, but not quite.

I'm grateful to the members of St. Peter's that we determined together to admit our difference, face our difficulties, work through our issues and find resolution. It wasn't an easy or painless process, but it was worth it. I admit there were Wednesdays when I looked forward to the weekly Employment Opportunities. There were congregations to which I sent my profile and some I interviewed with. But in the end, I decided to stay.

I grew up moving. Home was wherever the family was: four houses in four towns growing up, twenty three addresses total. I've served seven churches in two denominations in my career, and I've taken a decade out for secular employment between being a United Methodist pastor and being a United Church of Christ pastor. Moving comes easy for me; staying is what is hard.

Like any other career person, pastors move for a variety of reasons: better opportunity, larger congregations, living in a different part of the country, specialized ministry on a staff, to be near one's family or other family considerations, etc. Any reason that applies in a secular career also applies to clergy. We may not like to admit to building our careers or serving our egos, but it happens. We also move out of a profound sense of call, an inner compulsion that cannot be described any better than it can be resisted; we are called and do have a call. We also move physically because, deep down, we simply can't stand staying where we are spiritually.

A friend once said, "If you can't change people, just change people." What she meant was, when you can't change the way some people are, find a different set of people to associate with. The self-care of any pastor requires us to consider when we have been called to a congregation and when we have been called away. Not every congregation is at a place in its life where it's willing or able to become a healing place rather than a hurting place. Too often the pastor serves as lightning rod and sacrificial lamb, the biblical scapegoat. Sometimes it does become necessary for us to move on. It's important to our integrity that when we decide it is time to move on, it's not simply to feed our ego. We need to discern God's leading us in our staying and in our going, in our holding and in our folding.

I hope that I am encouraging my fellow pastors to stay put, to do the tough work and run the risks, to get help, and to grow where you are planted, if at all possible.

MEDITATION

Remember your first sense of being called into parish ministry. Remember the process you went through in discerning the genuineness of that call. Remember the questions and the soul searching. Was there anxiety? How did you resolve it? Was there uncertainty? How did you clarify it?

Now remember the last time you considered a call to a particular congregation, whether you accepted it or not. How was this process similar to the former one? How was it different? How much of the consideration was of a divine call and how much was personal desire?

QUESTIONS FOR REFLECTION AND DISCUSSION

1. What were the issues and concerns that led to your last move from your previous congregation? What various factors were parts of your decision? Did you follow a process of discernment? If so, describe it.

2. When was the last time you had serious thoughts about taking a different call? What prompted you to consider the change?

3. If you were not a pastor, what would you do? What other interests do you have? What other profession matches your interests and abilities?

4. How have the times that you have moved affected your spiritual life? How has choosing to stay affected your spiritual life?

12

A LONG WALK

Eugene Peterson, in his book *A Long Obedience in the Same Direction* (a quote from Nietzsche), says that genuine spirituality calls us to a long walk in a constant direction. Our personal spiritual growth comes more from staying put than it does from moving on. If we're going to go through the deep water and the raging storm, how do we keep ourselves afloat? If we're in over our heads with change we can't control, conflict we can't resolve, stress we can't manage and anxiety that is in the air we breathe, how do we keep our heads above water? How can we not only survive the storm but find a way to flourish and thrive?

Much has been written about clergy self-care; here is a summary. We're not to over-eat, we're to watch our carbohydrate intake, and we are to get regular exercise and a full night's sleep. We can't be any kind of "holic:" workaholic, alcoholic or engage in any other form of substance abuse. Balance time with work, family, hobbies, and maintain a devotional life independent of sermon or Bible study preparation. Keep a journal. Seek spiritual direction or companionship. Continue professional growth and education beyond seminary and throughout our career. Keep fresh, alive, interesting and interested. These are all basic guidelines we've read before; the discipline is in doing them.

Another discipline not often listed is maintaining a sense of perspective. It's easy to get caught up in the moment, especially when others are in crisis. The emotion can be infectious. The deodorant commercial used to say, "Never let them see you sweat," which is about outward appearance rather than inner calm Our

Buddhist brothers and sisters focus on maintaining a compassionate detachment, caring about others without owning their problems. "Compassionate detachment" is a critical term: we're called to a caring profession, as Christians we're called to love one another, even love our enemy. Yet we also realize we cannot do everything, we cannot be all things to all people. We need to care about others without attaching our egos to their issues. Bowen Family System theory has been applied to congregational life and speaks of self-differentiation, participating with a system while not becoming a part of it by being aware of and true to one's self.

Perspective also reminds us not to take things personally; it's not always all about us. Everyone has issues they're working on. We may just be the punching bag they are using to vent emotions about something else.

When a Roman general returned from conquest a triumphant parade was held in his honor. Riding a chariot in full regalia, the general would have a slave standing behind him, holding a wreath over the general's head and whispering in his ear, "*Sic transit Gloria,*" all glory is fleeting. This too shall pass.

It's good to remember, when we're on the top of our game, the top of the heap, the top of the world and everything is absolutely perfect, that this too shall pass. When we're in the depths of despair and everything has fallen apart like a house of cards; when all we've done is abject failure, this too shall pass.

If I could pick two ingredients most critical for surviving and thriving in a world of chaos and when a congregation in crisis, they wouldn't be diet or exercise, journaling or spiritual direction. They would be perseverance and perspective. Hang in there. Things will change.

I have friends who teach in the public schools. In the course of their careers they've seen massive changes. As they approach retirement, they've compared fellow teachers with each other. Some experienced thirty years of teaching and some experienced thirty times of teaching the same year over and over. As pastors, we may be tempted to move when we've preached ourselves out. We may move to a different congregation where we can preach the same sermons again. When we stay, we need to write fresh material and offer ourselves to be continually renewed.

My Ph.D. focused on Celtic pilgrimage as a model for living today. In this study, the images that emerged included: the joy is in the journey and life is a pilgrimage from the place of our birth to the place of our rising. If we are pilgrims, then we're on pilgrimage, which means life is about being on the way, not arriving. My mentor had me read a book entitled Staying Put, which took up the opposite theme. The author argued that we grow inwardly best when we're in a stable place outwardly. The advice might seem opposite, but the meaning is just as true.

A tree that is transplanted too often does not grow deep roots. Trees need stability to put down deep roots. Without deep roots, a tree can't spread out broad branches. Stability and growth need to maintain a balance that is vital and dynamic for the tree to grow and be healthy.

Some of the bravest people I know are the ones who stayed when it would have been easy to leave. Sometimes the greatest expression of faith is in just staying put.

MEDITATION

Remember a time when you felt happiest, successful, fulfilled. What were the outer circumstances that led to the inner sensation? Recall that feeling and hold on to it; it is always there, ready to be remembered.

Remember a time you felt like a failure, when you were in despair. What events fed those emotions? You can recall these feelings at will as well. Choose which you prefer to feel and hold on to that feeling.

QUESTIONS FOR REFLECTION AND DISCUSSION

1. What personal disciplines do you regularly follow? How have they proven helpful?

2. Review times you felt most stressed or conflicted. Were you able to maintain your personal disciplines during those times?

3. Share how maintaining a sense of perspective has been helpful in times of transition in your ministry.

4. How have the disciplines of perseverance and perspective played out in your spiritual life and in your ministry?

13

Spiritual Calisthenics

In my younger days I did a lot of working out: free weights, running, cross country skiing, even calisthenics while watching television. Like too many older athletes, the older I get, the better I was. I think you can compare spiritual disciplines with the disciplines of regular physical exercise.

The spiritual disciplines aren't meant for clergy or parish professionals alone. All Christians are urged, even expected, to have some form of spiritual discipline to help keep them on their path and to stimulate further growth. Pastors are called to be role models and to offer ourselves as examples for others to follow. In his classic *Celebration of Discipline: the Path to Spiritual Growth,* Richard Foster categorizes the exercises of spiritual discipline as inward, outward and corporate.

The inward disciplines include meditation, prayer, fasting and study. The Didache instructs us to pray the Lord's Prayer three times daily. The classical monastic formula is seven times of prayer daily: Matins, Lauds, Terce, Sext, None, Vespers and Compline, plus a daily Eucharist. Typically, I have morning and evening prayer times when I read prayers or a prayer office. In the morning, I have two prayers that include some body stretches. I will then set a timer for twenty minutes and meditate. Sitting comfortably, eyes closed, long slow deep steady breathes, focusing on my prayer word: "deep peace" or "Jesus." When the timer goes off, I offer an extended version of the Lord's Prayer. I keep a journal by my side and will make entries afterward. For several years, I read the Bible through annually. I read over thirty books every year. I try to maintain an active and regular practice of prayer and study; I am serious about the pursuit of holy wisdom! I used to fast Wednesdays and Fridays, but have not kept a regular pattern of fasting for some years and very much look it.

Throughout the day I will regularly do some deep breathing exercises. I take a long, slow, deep breath and pray the "Jesus Prayer:" "Lord Jesus Christ, son of God, have mercy on me, a sinner." Hold the breath and silently repeat the prayer. Then slowly release the breath, again repeating the prayer, until the lungs are empty. Feel that emptiness, that desire to breathe, while again repeating the prayer. This exercise helps me center and focus and is a great tension reliever.

The outward disciplines include simplicity, solitude, submission and service. For most of us, our role as clergy and the limits of our salaries help us maintain these disciplines. I like to shop thrift stores as much as possible. Becki likes to garden and recruits my help. Introverts especially need times of solitude. Introverts make up the majority of clergy, though our parishes would like us to be extroverts. In our United States society, introverts learn to act like extroverts. Henri Nouwen writes that we all need to balance our time between solitude and community.

To these outward disciplines I would add physical exercise. Most of us live very sedentary lives and we need to get up and move around more. Take a walk, mow the yard, pull weeds (you can even name them after people), ride a bike, go swimming. We can practice the discipline of four one syllable words: "eat less, move more." I have a mile and a half route I walk four times a week. Becki and I walk a mile or so three evenings a week. I don't normally walk Saturdays or Sundays: let the week-end be the week-end on Saturday and focus on worship on Sunday.

The corporate disciplines include confession, worship, guidance and celebration. I hope that we find times while we are leading worship that we can also engage ourselves in worship. I wrote in the previous chapter about the importance of spiritual direction or companionship, which would include both confession and guidance.

I've been asked how I survived through our time of conflict and testing. I remember that stress is constant and times of conflict are to be expected every three to five years and average, so we all go through it. Some of my survival is simply by default: I did seek other calls, but could not find another call where I'd rather be which also wanted me. I always had a core of support in the congregation; by June of 2008, after our crisis moment in November 2007, I felt general support from the majority of the membership. I have been fortunate to have the support of two local clergy groups: our local ecumenical group and our United Church of Christ cluster, which has been a lifesaver on several occasions for nearly all of us in it. The members of the Academy of Parish Clergy have been more helpful than they realize, just by being there and available.

I would add the gift and discipline of friendship. At a seminar for long term clergy, we were asked to list all our friends. We're then to eliminate all those who were members of the church we were then serving - they were members first and we dare never forget that. Eliminate members of previous churches; they would always think of us as "pastor" first. Eliminate all colleagues in ministry; they were potential rivals. At this point, most of us had no one left on the list, and none of us had more than a handful. I am blessed to have friends who know me as "Dave" rather than as pastor or colleague, friends who will joke with me, argue with me and listen to me, who have known me through the years and for who I used to be, and who will be with me through years to come. If you have one person you can call a true friend, you can survive. That fact has become increasingly important to me: if you have one person you can call a true friend, you can survive almost anything.

We all know this already. We know what the disciplines are and why we should practice them. This does not mean that we always do, myself included. If you're practicing these disciplines, good for you. If not, maybe a word to the wise is sufficient to motivate you to return to a regular pattern of physical and spiritual discipline.

MEDITATION

Imagine a vast and barren dessert, empty of life. Feel the dryness of the ground, the heat in the air, the sun beating down. Imagine being in that dessert. Now picture an oasis in the midst of the dessert: a pool of water, surrounded by green plants, shrubs and trees, fish swimming in the water and animals playing in the trees. Remember a time you felt like that dessert and how you managed to find your oasis.

QUESTIONS FOR REFLECTION AND DISCUSSION

1. What spiritual disciplines are you currently practicing? What is your pattern? How is it working? What is your accountability?

2. Eliminating all current and former members and all fellow clergy, who do you have on your friends list? How do you maintain those relationships? When was the last time you had an in-depth conversation with one of them?

14

FINDING FAITH WHEN EVERYTHING IS LOST

Mom was driving along the highway with my little brother Joe riding with her in the car. It was in the days before mandatory shoulder and safety belts or child restraint seats. A semi was approaching from the opposite direction. Mom thought the semi was encroaching into her lane; she swerved to miss it, went into the ditch and rolled the car. It was totaled, Joe had a broken leg and Mom was emotionally traumatized.

I share this because this is exactly where many clergy and their congregations seem to be finding themselves. They're living in that moment between swerving and crashing, while everything around us is tossing and turning, spinning and rolling and everything that isn't fastened down has come loose. We're not in charge and it appears no one else is either.

We're like Sinbad, who anchors his ship to an island only to discover that the island is a giant fish that now has his ship in tow. More appropriately, we're caught between Augustine and Pelagius, watching our world collapse around us. Augustine was born and raised in a benevolent world of a Christian Empire, but watched the Eternal city of Rome sacked by barbarians and his world fall into chaos. Pelagius lived in that same world, but as a Celtic monk he wasn't attached to the earthly empire. The two saw the same world from radically different perspectives. Augustine was a bishop; Pelagius was a monk. We know who won that power play, but we would do well to learn a lesson from Pelagius about things transient and things eternal.

The world is a changing place and the rate of change is constantly accelerating. What we thought we knew no longer seems to be true. Outside our congregations is a raging storm in a sea of change. Inside our congregations we've hunkered down desperately trying to hold on. Anxiety turns to fear and stress, which turns to despair, which turns to gritty determination or exhausted resignation. Where is our hope?

This is the question that clergy face as they seek to minister and lead in a world of constant change. When all seems lost, where can we hold fast? Remember to seek balance in the change rather than stability against the change. We cannot control the change in the culture or the conflict in our congregations; we can manage ourselves. Remember persistence and perspective: hang in there, things will change!

When I felt I was losing everything, I remembered the example of Julian of Norwich. She was a single homeless woman in fourteenth century England. We're not even sure of her name. Medieval Europe was not a good time for a woman to be alone. England was being torn apart by a civil war and devastated by the plague. Julian built a hovel against the cathedral wall in Durham. She caught a fever and nearly died. During the delirium of her fever, she had a series of visions. When she recovered, she recorded her visions in her book *Showings: Revelations of Divine Love.* This book, written by a single woman, sick and homeless during war and plague, is summarized in her statement, "All will be well and all will be well and all manner of things will be well."

I still get choked up writing it. When I felt my world falling apart and all hell breaking loose; with nowhere to go, no place to hide, nothing to hold on to, I would remember Julian in her delirium and remind myself, "All will be well and all will be well and all manner of things will be well." I had no idea how things would work out. I only knew that they would.

When we feel helpless and the situation seems hopeless, we can still confess that all will be well!

Someone said the church today is a lot like Noah's ark: if it weren't for the storm outside, you couldn't stand the stink inside.

Paul writes "We exult even in our trials and tribulations, for they develop perseverance, perseverance develops character, character brings us hope, and our hope does not disappoint us, for the love of God has been poured into our hearts through the Holy Spirit who has been given to us" (Romans 5:3-5).

Yes, we're facing a storm of change. Yes, it's beyond our control and even our understanding. Yes, our congregations are affected and infected by the stress, anxiety and dysfunctionality. But we're not helpless and our cause is not hopeless. We of all people have hope!

There is in each of our congregations a vital and dynamic core, a central still point, a sure foundation that is steadfast and unwavering, that has stood the test of time over millennia. It may lie buried beneath the trappings of the past decades' traditions, but it is still there. We can uncover this treasure and use it as a landmark to guide us through to the other side.

History has demonstrated that the church is always at its greatest internal strength when it's in the direst external circumstances.

In 30 CE the one Christians hail as master and teacher was brutally tortured and executed, his body placed in a borrowed tomb. Even after the Resurrection, the disciples huddled secretly in an upper room. Fifty days later, those cowering disciples burst forth from that upper room courageously proclaiming what they called Good News of the love of God for all people: Jew and Gentile, male and female, slave and free, even Greek and Roman. In the words of their former antagonists, they turned the world upside down.

In the following centuries, the church suffered persecution, was decried as atheists and anarchists, and yet the more they were persecuted, the more they grew in numbers. Tertullian would write, "The blood of the martyrs is the seed of the church." The church responded to the oppressive attacks with acts of loving kindness and mercy. The Roman philosophers were defenseless to such acts of grace and could only respond, "My, how these Christians love one another!" In four centuries, the church grew from a small group hiding out in Jerusalem to a force that converted the Empire from pagan to Christian, conquering without killing though being killed, using only the force of its faith.

Through the following centuries the church faced both internal and external threats, and found renewed strength in its response. The establishment of a proto-Catholic church in the Nicene Councils provided structure for the spiritual energy of the early church, yet also excluded the earliest Monophysite churches of Egypt, Syria, Mesopotamia and Armenia. Still, the spirit of faith was made evident through the desert fathers and mothers and the Greek mystics of Mt. Athos and elsewhere. When the Crusades waged a war of bloodshed and violence throughout the land three religions call "Holy," a young man in Assisi stripped himself of everything but his faith and dedicated his life to rebuilding the church. Francis has a following that continues to this day, while the crusaders lie moldering in their graves. Pope Leo X dreamed of an earthly building that would reflect the heavenly glory of God in the name of St. Peter's and a monk and priest nailed his ninety-five theses to the door of Wittenberg's church protesting the indulgences. On trial for his life, he confessed "Here I stand, God help me, I can do no other." Martin Luther inspired a Reformation that gave birth to an entirely new expression of the Christian faith in Protestantism and, by its influence, inspired a counter-reformation that renewed the Catholic Church.

The church has faced storms without and conflict within and, every time, the church has survived, the church has thrived, the church has triumphed. It has often been messy and sometimes painful. What seems divisive at the time may lead to multiplying expressions of the faith. I do not know what the church will look like on the other side of the current cultural shifts. I can't see the final goal. I can take the next step. Others speculate on Emergent Christianity, Progressive Christianity and the church of the third millennium. I am confident that there will be a church!

Life demands more than I can supply. That's okay; it's not about me. Church membership, worship attendance, church school, youth, Christian education attendance, giving are all down, while population increases. That's okay; it is not about the survival of my local congregation. On a global scale, Christianity is the world's largest religion, accounting for a third of the world's population. It continues to expand in South America, Africa and Asia. Within my lifetime, China is expected to have the largest Christian population of any country on the planet. I will die, my congregation may fade, but the faith will endure.

We're not helpless and we're not hopeless. Our confidence is not in ourselves alone. Over and again, we're reminded our help is in the Lord; our hope is in our God. Hope does not disappoint us. Hebrews describes hope as an anchor, sure and steadfast. Faith may be founded upon the past, what we've experienced and learned, but hope comes to us from the future. It may be a future we can't see, it might be a future we won't reach, but it is real nonetheless.

The ship of the church may be tossed about by the storms around it, but the anchor is set firm and will bring us through. What we see as most urgent may not be what's truly important. "The things that are seen are temporary; the things that are unseen are eternal" (2 Corinthians 4:18). The storm will pass, as they always have and always will. The ship will survive, provided we focus on what is most real and most lasting.

MEDITATION

Recall the lessons learned from church history: trials and tribulation, persecutions and divisions. Consider the triumphs and failures of previous generations and how they came through those times. Remember difficult days you have faced, times that were uncertain and a future unseen. Consider how you survived those days to arrive at a better place in your life.

QUESTIONS FOR REFLECTION AND DISCUSSION

1. Review the paragraphs on church history: triumphs and tragedies, distractions, divisions, difficulties. How were those crises handled? What would it have been like to live through those times?

2. What is your sense of the future of the global church? Where is there growth and hope, where conflict and testing?

3. Can you apply lessons from church history or from the global church to your local congregation? Do these other instances give a sense of perspective?

4. Julian of Norwich had several strikes against her in fourteenth century England: a woman, alone, homeless, feverish, during plague and a civil war, yet she was able to say, "All will be well, and all will be well, and all manner of things will be well." Her witness helped me in my struggles. Can you relate her struggles to your own?

15

A COMMUNITY OF THE BELOVED

It's my personal belief, my strong conviction, my guiding light and sustaining strength, that the essence, core, center, foundation, treasure of our faith can be summarized in one word - love. Our congregation is called to be a community of the beloved, where the love of God is made known and lived out in tangible, practical and concrete ways, where we make the eternal truth our incarnate reality.

Jesus offers the love of God as the first and greatest commandment, the love of neighbor and of self as the second commandment, "like unto the first," making the first commandment tangible. As the new commandment, he asks us to love one another even as he loves us, "greater love has no one than this: to lay down one's life for one's friends."

For most of my life I have made few friends. A friend is one for whom I am willing to die. One who I grew to call "friend" offered a different slant: a friend is someone who makes your life worth living. That's in the positive, a good affirmation; I want more of those friends!

I imagine our congregation gathered for morning worship, with all kinds of people of all shapes, sizes, descriptions, appearances, pasts and perspectives. I can see someone scooting over in their pew, not wanting to get to close, and then reaching over to this stranger, whispering, "I don't like you, I don't know you, I don't understand you, but in the name of Christ I am willing to die for you." A congregation with that kind of love will have the courage to find the understanding and appreciation of each of us in our differences. Jesus challenges us to say with Job, "Even though he slay me, yet shall I love him!" (Job 13:15)

Paul writes that love fulfills the Law, and is a debt none of us can fully repay. He describes love as the greatest of all gifts and lists it as the first of the fruits of the Spirit. John tells us that God is love and that God's love is made complete in us (1 John 4:7-12).

I imagine a congregation that has grounded itself in the love of God: in their personal experience of a loving God, a God who loves them with an unconditional and irresistible love, a God who then loves others in and through their love of one another; a congregation where the love of God is made manifest.

This congregation will still have differences; there will still be disagreements, debates, even arguments. We are each of us unique, with our own pasts, preferences, priorities and perspectives. We will begin, end and ground our gatherings on the Shaker greeting: "The Christ in me greets the Christ in thee and draws us together in love." If it is the love of God that unites us, there is no power on this earth that can successfully divide us.

This love is the foundation of our faith. It's the source of our wisdom, the tether that bind us together, the guiding light before us, the order for our worship, and the agenda for our meetings. This love invites us to offer extravagant welcome, inspires us to heights of extraordinary worship and encourages us to give exemplary witness. This love is the power that propels us forward through the dark night. This love lit the fire that drove the first disciples out of the upper room and into the streets at Pentecost, that emboldened the martyrs before blazing flames and ravenous beasts, that called Francis to joyous poverty, that spoke freedom through the mouth of Martin Luther, and that will get us through our own difficulties.

Our image of the love of God is sometimes too stiff and formal, overly intellectualized. We imagine God as a kindly grandparent, doting over the grandkids. I think of God as our passionate lover, who is in love with us. God is like that 13 year old adolescent, filled with passion for their new-found love. God is like the 21 year old, full of life and energy, hope and promise, wanting to share all of life with their beloved. I remember my first love as an adolescent, how it drove me as if I were possessed. I know the power of that emotion was only infatuation, not a deep and lasting love, but I still know the power of that emotion. I think God is that powerfully in love with us: the God who is love is in love with us as the beloved. Our churches are the places on this earth where this amazing, eternal love is found, is experienced, is made real and lived out. Each of us is part of a community of the beloved!

When we remember this, for it is the treasure of the ages from the life of the faithful that lies buried beneath the trappings of our traditions, we will find the truth that Pierre Teilhard de Chardin describes, "Someday, after mastering the wind and waves, tides and gravity, we shall harness for God the energies of love, and then, for the second time in the history of the world, we will have discovered fire."

MEDITATION

Remember a time you felt most loved, remember all the feelings involved in that experience. Remember who was involved; remember what events led to it. Remember that love!

Remember a time you felt love for another, not infatuation or physical attraction, but a love that wanted only the best for the other, love that was willing to give itself in love. Remember the force and authority of that love.

Remember a time when someone embodied for you the love of God. Remember a time when you were able to embody God's love for another. Remember the experience and the emotion, and the sense of fulfillment personally and professionally.

QUESTIONS FOR REFLECTION AND CONVERSATION

1. How can our congregations grow in their experience of love? How can they improve in their expression of love? What are some examples of love?

2. Reflecting on your early loves, what can they teach you of God's love?

3. Frederick Buechner describes our calling as the place where our greatest gladness and the world's greatest need meet. What is your experience of this?

4. St. Brigit of Ireland says "A soul without a friend is like a body without a head." Who have been friends for your soul? How have you experienced the divine presence through your relationship with them?

16

WORTH IT ALL

It was a Monday evening in May, 2012. I was sitting in the fellowship hall of a sister congregation, waiting to meet with their church council. Along with another pastor, I'd been asked to come, meet with them and share our story. They were facing some issues of congregational conflict.

Their previous pastor had left under a cloud; not all members were made aware of the circumstances. They decided to arrange weekly pulpit supply rather than an intentional interim, which led to an accelerated and abbreviated search process. The new pastor felt accepted, but also felt like he kept hitting invisible walls emotionally around key members of the church. To help with this, he was taking some continuing professional education aimed at parish revitalization.

At a recent congregational meeting, their youth director and council president nearly came to blows. It was a loud and angry exchange. Afterward, nobody wanted to talk about what had just taken place; they wanted to bury it and move on, acting as if nothing had happened and everything had returned to normal.

The pastor had invited the two of us guest clergy because we'd each gone through similar difficulties in the churches we were serving, and seemed to be the better for it. After listening to the council members share their perceptions of the past few years, we each shared our stories.

Our churches faced issues. There had been an emotionally violent eruption, with threats of dividing the congregation. People were furious and frightened, not knowing how to move forward.

The pastor stayed, the church leadership decided to face and deal with the congregation's issues. Consultants were brought in, training took place, several congregational meetings were held. It was tough work. It carried a cost, financially and emotionally. In the long run, it was all worth it. Each congregation was better for it, stronger and wiser, had moved from reticent to resilient. Each congregation was a happier, healthier and more honest place to be.

We offered our support, urging them to confront their issues, deal with them, and learn from them. Move from reticence to resilience. We need more resilient congregations, congregations who have grown through their issues and become stronger and healthier for it. We need congregations that are "glad" rather than "sad," that seek balance rather than stability, that encourage persistence and perspective.

I sat through that meeting, listening to each person share their fears and concerns, their hopes. I reflected on what we'd been through, how we had learned and grown from our experiences.

I am glad to be where I'm at. I'm grateful for the people at St. Peter's who believed in me enough to sign the petition urging me to stay. I'm glad the members believed in themselves, and their church, enough to take the risk and make the effort to grow with their pastor. I'm glad we swallowed hard, bit the bullet and hired the consultant. It proved to be money well spent. I'm grateful for all my fellow clergy who stood with me, supporting me, through our troubles. I appreciate the people who cared, the members who shared their own heartaches and disappointments and had faith enough in the process to open them up in ways they'd not been able to previously. We have weathered the storm, we have navigated the shoals. Now we're in a good place. The future looks bright and the wind is at our backs.

We have gone from being stressed, anxious and dysfunctional, using specific practical and actionable methods to become a resilient congregation. To be resilient means that we are flexible and adaptable, we can recover from pressure and shock undamaged, we are capable of springing back after being stretched or compressed.

We may be knocked down, but we will always get back up. We've gone from being a congregation at risk to being a congregation known for its resilience.

In another recent self-study, our sense of purpose as a congregation and our optimism for the future both scored very strongly. We know who we are and we know where we are going. We are a resilient congregation! And I'm a grateful pastor.

MEDITATION

What has been the best moment of your clergy career? How did that day feel? Remember what led up to that moment and the after-glow that followed. Enjoy that moment, cherish it well.

QUESTIONS FOR REFLECTION AND CONVERSATION

1. What is your greatest hope for the congregation you are now serving? What signs of promise do you see on the horizon?

2. What would you attempt if you knew you could not fail?

3. It's been said that the strongest trees grow in the most exposed places. How have the issues you've confronted and struggled with in your congregations served to strengthen you spiritually?

RE-ORIENTATION

It has been an exhilarating experience: from risk to resilience, from the passing storm to the lasting peace, from temporary troubles to a lasting love. If this book has been effective, we will have re-oriented ourselves. We will have remembered who, and whose, we are. We will have adjusted, adapted and are ready to overcome. Our situation in this new and ever-changing culture is the same, but our attitude is different. We will know our position on the path and be confident in our direction. The passage remains treacherous, but we have a landmark to fix upon and guide our passing. We will have set ourselves and our congregations in accordance with our culture and in agreement with our call to be faithful witnesses of our enduring faith in our time and place.

I hope that you will enjoy your journey!

MEDITATION

Remember the section of this book that most inspired you in the reading. What was that section? Remember the feeling. The experience passes, but the remembering endures.

QUESTIONS FOR REFLECTION AND CONVERSATION

1. What idea in the book did you find most challenging? Most promising? Most encouraging? Most confusing or frustrating?

2. What will you take from this book as a practice in your congregation? What will you be able to apply to your life?

Bibliography

Bass, Diana Butler. *Christianity for the Rest of Us: How the Neighborhood Church is Transforming the Faith.* San Francisco: Harper One Publishers, 2006.

Bellah, Robert N., et. al. *Habits of the Heart: Individualism and Commitment in American Life.* New York: Harper and Row Publishers, 1985.

Borg, Marcus. *The Heart of Christianity: Rediscovering a Life of Faith.* San Francisco: Harper One Publishers, 2003.

Brown, Juanita with David Isaacs. *The World Café: Shaping our Futures Through Conversations That Matter.* San Francisco: Berrett-Koehler Publishers, 2005.

Campolo, Tony. *Red Letter Christians: A Citizen's Guide to Faith and Politics.* Ventura: Regal Books, 2008.

Collins, Jim. *Built to Last: Successful Habits of Visionary Companies.* New York: Collins Business, 2002.

_____. *Good to Great: Why Some Companies Make the Leap and Others Don't.* New York: Harper Business, 2001.

_____. *How the Mighty Fall and Why Some Companies Never Give In.* Boulder: Jim Collins. 2009.

Crabb, Lawrence. *Real Church: Does it Exist? Can I Find It?* Nashville: Thomas Nelson, 2009.

Dean, William. *The American Spiritual Culture: And the Invention of Jazz, Football and the Movies.* New York: Continuum Publishing, 2003.

Easum, William. *Sacred Cows Make Gourmet Burgers: Ministry Anytime Anywhere by Anyone.* Nashville: Abingdon Press, 1995.

Friedman, Edwin. *A Failure of Nerve: Leadership in the Age of the Quick Fix.* Harrisburg: Seabury Books, 2007.

Goodman, Denise W. *Congregational Fitness: Healthy Practices for Layfolk.* Herndon, VA: The Alban Institute, 2000.

Hamilton, Adam. *Leading Beyond the Walls: Developing Congregations with a Heart for the Unchurched.* Nashville: Abingdon Press, 2002.

Hauerwas, Stanley and William H. Willimon. *Resident Aliens: Life in the Christian Colony.* Nashville: Abingdon Press, 1989.

Healy, Anthony E. *The Postindustrial Promise: Vital Religious Community in the 21ˢᵗ Century.* Herndon, VA: The Alban Institute, 2005.

Herrington, Jim, et. al. *Leading Congregational Change: A Practical Guide for the Transformational Journey.* San Francisco: Jossey-Bass, 2000.

Jenkins, Philip. *The Next Christendom: The Coming of Global Christianity.* New York: Oxford University Press, 2002.

Kinnamon, David and Gabe Lyons. *Unchristian: What a New Generation Really Thinks about Christianity and Why it Matters.* Grand Rapids: Baker Books, 2007.

McClaren, Brian D. *More Ready than you Realize: Evangelism as Dance in the Postmodern Matrix.* Grand Rapids: Zondervan, 2002.

_____. *The Secret Message of Jesus: Uncovering the Truth that could Change Everything.* Nashville: Thomas Nelson Publishers. 2006.

Mead, Loren B. *The Once and Future Church Collection: Reinventing the Church for a New Mission Frontier, Transforming Congregations for the Future, Five Challenges for the Once and Future Church.* Herndon, VA: The Alban Institute, 2001.

Merritt, Carol Howard. *Reframing Hope: Vital Ministry in a New Generation.* Herndon, VA: The Alban Institute, 2010.

_____. *Tribal Church: Ministering to the Missing Generation.* Herndon: The Alban Institute, 2007.

Miller, Donald. Blue Like Jazz: *Nonreligious Thoughts on Christian Spirituality.* Nashville: Thomas Nelson Publishers, 2003.

Nixon, Paul. *I Refuse to Serve a Dying Church.* Cleveland: Pilgrim Press. 2007.

Prothero, Stephen. *American Jesus: How the Son of God Became a National Icon.* New York: Farrar, Straus and Giroux, 2003.

Putnam, Robert D. *Bowling Alone: The Collapse and Revival of American Community.* New York: Simon and Schuster, 2001.

Rainer, Thom S. *Surprising Insights from the Unchurched and Proven Ways to Reach Them.* Grand Rapids: Zondervan, 2001.

Rendle, Gilbert R. *Behavioral Covenants in the Congregation: A Handbook for Honoring Differences.* Herndon, VA: The Alban Institute. 1999.

_____. *Leading Change in the Congregation: Spiritual and Organizational Tools for Leaders.* Herndon: The Alban Institute, 1998.

_____. *Living into the New World: How Cultural Trends Affect Your Congregation: an Alban Institute Video.* Herndon: The Alban Institute, 2001.

Rendle, Gil and Alice Mann. *Holy Conversations: Strategic Planning as a Spiritual Practice for Congregations.* Herndon: The Alban Institute, 2003.

Richio, David. *Five Things We Cannot Change: And the Happiness We Find by Embracing Them.* Boston: Shambhala Publications. 2006.

Robinson, Anthony B. *Leadership for Vital Congregations.* Cleveland: Pilgrim Press. 2006.

_____. *It's a Whole New World. Internet Course.* www.ucc.org.

_____. *Transforming Congregational Culture.* Grand Rapids: Wm B. Eerdmans Publishing Co., 2003.

Roof, Wade Clark. *Spiritual Marketplace: Baby Boomers and the Remaking of American Religion.* Princeton: Princeton University Press. 1999.

Schnase, Robert. *Five Practices of Fruitful Congregations.* Nashville: Abingdon Press, 2007.

Smith, Daniel P. and Mary K. Sellon. *Pathway to Renewal: Practical Steps for Congregations.* Herndon: The Alban Institute, 2008.

Spong, John Shelby. *A New Christianity for a New World: Why Traditional Faith is Dying and How a New Faith is Being Born.* San Francisco: Harper Collins Publishers, 2001.

Steinke, Peter L. *A Door Set Open: Grounding Change in Mission and Hope.* Herndon: Alban Institute, 2010.

_____. *Congregational Leadership in Anxious Times: Being Calm and Courageous No Matter What.* Herndon: The Alban Institute. 2006.

_____. *Healthy Congregations: A Systems Approach.* Herndon: The Alban Institute. 1996.

_____. *How Your Church Family Works: Understanding Congregations as Emotional Systems.* Herndon VA: The Alban Institute, 1993.

Tickle, Phyllis. *The Great Emergence: How Christianity is Changing and Why.* Grand Rapids: Baker Publishing Group, 2008.

Wheatley, Margaret J. *Leadership and the New Science: Discovering Order in a Chaotic World.* San Francisco: Barrett-Koehler Publishers, 1999.

Also from Energion Publications and the Academy of Parish Clergy

Conversations in Ministry
Edited by: Robert D. Cornwall

Clergy Table Talk
Kent Ira Groff

... a must read for pastors who want to balance effectiveness with spiritual growth and personal well-being.
Bruce Epperly, Ph.D.

Coming May 2013 by David Moffett-Moore

In a wide ranging philosophical exploration, Moffett-Moore invites us to approach pilgrimage as the essence of existence rather than a religious event.

James Mulholland
Author of *If Grace is True* and *Praying like Jesus*

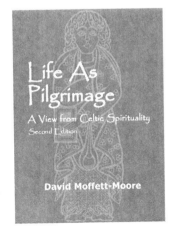

Life As Pilgrimage
A View from Celtic Spirituality
Second Edition

David Moffett-Moore

MORE FROM ENERGION PUBLICATIONS

Personal Study

Finding My Way in Christianity	Herold Weiss	$16.99
Holy Smoke! Unholy Fire	Bob McKibben	$14.99
The Jesus Paradigm	David Alan Black	$17.99
When People Speak for God	Henry Neufeld	$17.99
The Sacred Journey	Chris Surber	$11.99

Christian Living

Faith in the Public Square	Robert D. Cornwall	$16.99
Grief: Finding the Candle of Light	Jody Neufeld	$8.99
Crossing the Street	Robert LaRochelle	$16.99

Bible Study

Learning and Living Scripture	Lentz/Neufeld	$12.99
From Inspiration to Understanding	Edward W. H. Vick	$24.99
Luke: A Participatory Study Guide	Geoffrey Lentz	$8.99
Philippians: A Participatory Study Guide	Bruce Epperly	$9.99
Ephesians: A Participatory Study Guide	Robert D. Cornwall	$9.99

Theology

Creation in Scripture	Herold Weiss	$12.99
Creation: the Christian Doctrine	Edward W. H. Vick	$12.99
The Politics of Witness	Allan R. Bevere	$9.99
Ultimate Allegiance	Robert D. Cornwall	$9.99
History and Christian Faith	Edward W. H. Vick	$9.99
The Church Under the Cross	William Powell Tuck	$11.99
The Journey to the Undiscovered Country	William Powell Tuck	$9.99
Eschatology: A Participatory Study Guide	Edward W. H. Vick	$9.99

Ministry

Clergy Table Talk	Kent Ira Groff	$9.99
Out of This World	Darren McClellan	$24.99

Generous Quantity Discounts Available
Dealer Inquiries Welcome
Energion Publications — P.O. Box 841
Gonzalez, FL_ 32560
Website: http://energionpubs.com
Phone: (850) 525-3916

CPSIA information can be obtained
at www.ICGtesting.com
Printed in the USA
FFOW02n0452080514
5284FF